The Authority of Publius

The Authority of Publius

A READING OF THE FEDERALIST PAPERS

Albert Furtwangler

Cornell University Press

ITHACA AND LONDON

First published 1984 by Cornell University Press.
Published in the United Kingdom by Cornell University Press Ltd., London.

Acknowledgment is made to Wesleyan University Press for permission to quote excerpts from *The Federalist*, edited by Jacob E. Cooke; copyright © 1961 by Wesleyan University Press; reprinted from *The Federalist* by permission of Wesleyan University Press.

International Standard Book Number 0–8014–1643–4
Library of Congress Catalog Card Number 83–18806
Printed in the United States of America
Librarians: Library of Congress cataloging information appears on the last page of the book.

The paper in this book is acid-free and meets the guidelines for permanence and durability of the Committee on Production Guidelines for Book Longevity of the Council on Library Resources.

For Ginny, Tom, and Andy

Contents

Preface
9

CHAPTER ONE
An Idealized Argument
17

CHAPTER TWO
The Form of the *Federalist*
45

CHAPTER THREE
The Authority of Publius
80

CHAPTER FOUR
An Outcry against Literate Civility
98

CHAPTER FIVE
Shifting Contexts of *Federalist* No. 10
112

Conclusion
146

Index
149

Preface

The *Federalist* papers have long been esteemed as a classic of American politics and history. My aim in this brief book is to reassess these papers by looking closely at their form—by recognizing the literary strategies that shape their arguments and the conventions of political journalism which give meaning to the series as a whole.

To be fully understood, any piece of writing has to be seen against a background of formal conventions. When we study literature we usually keep these conventions in mind and look at a sonnet as a sonnet, a tragedy as a tragedy. But before other kinds of writing we are apt to relax our concentration and look for ideas or direct information without paying much attention to form. In fact, one of the strong appeals of modern journalism is that it invites us to suspend such critical awareness. We are accustomed to reading newspapers and magazines and tuning in news broadcasts in order to get brief but reliable information about current public issues. We read and listen according to the subtly flattering convention that we are learning without studying, absorbing precise information without exercising active critical judgment. We put our faith in the authority of journalists and their editors and focus our attention on the issues themselves, seldom stopping to think about the rhetoric and structure of the reports we are taking in. Only if we make a conscious effort—or are confronted with a striking discrepancy—do we realize that a "documentary" report is organized to persuade us to a journalist's personal point of view.

This habit of mind for reading journalism may explain in part why the *Federalist* has often been accepted as a direct report, a reliable newspaper series in which members of the Philadelphia Convention made a public account of the Constitution on the eve of its adoption. We now know that Alexander Hamilton, James Madison, and John Jay wrote these essays, and we sometimes consult them for that reason, expecting to find handy summaries of the authors' constitutional philosophies. Or we return to individual essays with a particular question in mind: What did these Founders have to say about Congressional representation, checks and balances, or a bill of rights?

But all such readings fail to do justice to the *Federalist*. In the first place, the series was neither designed nor originally understood as a neutral account. The papers were part of a vigorous debate, and they often appeared on the same pages as rival essays that attacked the Constitution and sharply questioned the motives and maneuvers of its proponents. Furthermore, one cannot grasp the main ideas of the *Federalist* by reading it only in part, in selected essays that stress certain constitutional topics. It is true that the series consists of eighty-five separate essays, which first ran in New York newspapers and then came out in a two-volume collection. But modern reprintings have often distorted or suppressed the ambiguities of that original form— to produce highly selective popular editions, papers sharply segregated because of different authorship, anthologized single numbers, and even condensations into excerpts-and-commentary. Even more vexing is the problem of authorship. In memoranda that Hamilton seems to have sanctioned many years later, he identified the authors of the various papers as he remembered them; but Madison provided a significantly different set of ascriptions; and the resulting conflict has remained unsolved for almost two centuries. Thus even the most critical and alert reader faces daunting puzzles from the outset. Is the page he is reading Hamilton's or Madison's, or one author's as reshaped by the other? Is the argument at hand part of a coherent book; or is it framed by a compact, timely essay; or is it part of a neat essay sequence—beginning and ending where? There may never be a way of reaching an unequivocal answer to these basic questions.

To address these problems I began by outlining all of the *Federalist* papers for myself, questioning whether they straightforwardly endorse the Constitution, and tracing out other lines of coherence suggested within them. I came to these papers after studying other periodical essay series of the eighteenth century and noticing some comparable devices in their rhetoric. But the particular features of the *Federalist* forced me to look further. I am now persuaded that this series modified the tradition of eighteenth-century newspaper campaigning, and so marked an important turn in the way constitutional questions could be posed before a large public.

Hence the authority of "Publius." Hamilton and Madison began with that safe and reassuring pseudonym for a few letters to the press. But the name came to encompass their collaborative talents as they extended them in remarkable new forms of argument. The present book is the intellectual biography of the composite figure that grew behind that signature. The first chapter reviews and challenges older approaches to the *Federalist* that disregard literary strategies. The second traces the development of the series and explains how Publius gave a special character and coherence to its arguments. The central chapter makes a case for the most outstanding qualities I see in the series as a whole. The remaining chapters test its strengths by looking into a different kind of contemporary argument, and by balancing various modern ways of interpreting the most famous paper, No. 10. Throughout these chapters I have tried to survey the large outline of the *Federalist* for readers who might well be put off by its seeming remoteness, technicality, or confusing arrangement. A reader must be patient and tolerant toward Publius; he frankly insists on such indulgence because of the hard political questions he addresses. But a modern reader needs help in meeting Publius on these terms. I have tried to create a framework that will reveal the dimensions of this rhetorical character: its historical setting, its depths, and its limitations.

This book has evolved over a period of years and it owes many of its merits to others. My teachers on constitutional matters—Sally Bryan, Benjamin Ziegler, Cushing Strout, and Barbara A. Black—have all contributed more than they know. Leslie Brisman, Kenneth Ericksen, and Arthur Kimball have given me friendly support as I have worked at successive versions on their campuses, Yale and Linfield College. My colleague William Godfrey has lent me books and answered odd queries about early American history. Parts of Chapters One and Two have had the benefit of presentation in *Early American Literature* (1979) and at the Portland Area Literary Conference at Pacific University (1980). I have taken advantage of very thoughtful criticisms by two anonymous readers for Cornell University

Press. The responsibility for remaining defects is mine alone.

For very courteous help with their collections I am indebted to the New-York Historical Society, the American Antiquarian Society, and the libraries of Yale University. The staff of the Mount Allison University Library has been unfailingly helpful. A research grant from the Marjorie Young Bell Fund enabled me to begin a first draft during a sabbatical leave as Visiting Fellow at Yale (1977–78). Faculty research funds at Mount Allison have aided subsequent research.

Two wider circumstances also call for acknowledgment. The text and notes cite a number of modern studies and editions of the *Federalist*—studies that I have sometimes subjected to close questioning. It will be obvious to any careful reader that I have built on a great deal of recent work by others, that in fact I could never have begun without it. I have also learned much about the subject of this book by living in Canada during the past decade, and witnessing daily debates about the emergence of another federal constitution on this continent.

My wife has not typed this manuscript, nor has she read it. She has provided invaluable companionship, however, by working on books of her own, and invaluable support in countless other ways.

ALBERT FURTWANGLER

Sackville, New Brunswick

The Authority of Publius

CHAPTER ONE

An Idealized Argument

The *Federalist* papers deserve better reading than they usually get. As they have been understood throughout American history, they are authoritative papers on the Constitution. Most of them were written by Alexander Hamilton and James Madison, two of the leading spirits behind the Philadelphia Convention. These same authors became important statesmen in the early years of the republic. The *Federalist* appeared during the ratification debates, and it comprises an extensive discussion of constitutional matters; it presents cogent reasons for the adoption that actually took place. Taken singly, many of the papers still invite close study for what they say about federalism, representative government, checks and balances, judicial review, and guarantees of human rights. Altogether they have been taken as seminal writings of the Founders, ranking just after the Declaration of Independence and the Constitution itself as explanations of the shape of American politics and institutions.

The problem with such a good reputation, of course, is that it can blind us to other intrinsic merits in these writings. In good eighteenth-century parlance, the *Federalist* papers suffer from prescriptive veneration. They carry an enormous weight of authority. For two centuries they have stood behind the growth and survival of American political life. They seem to summarize the background of American successes and ideals. To put it directly: they have held the place of a compact, articulate American political theory. I believe that these papers deserve a great authority, but that the usual terms for praising them actually obscure much of their real importance.

In my view, the *Federalist* does not turn out to be very satisfying as an account of the United States government—currently, historically, or ideally. I believe that the kinds of authority suggested in my opening paragraph are all vulnerable to close analysis. Taken singly, none of them provides sufficient grounds for the great reputation of the *Federalist*. And even when weighed together they leave out an essential dimension of its enduring importance.

The closer one looks at these papers, the more they reflect a timely approach to a very particular occasion. They are unique among the arguments over ratification. But along with many other arguments for and against the Constitution, they share a commonplace eighteenth-century form. They are essays in a series, published anonymously or pseudonymously in the regular newspapers of a sizable city. This form is so commonplace, so prosaic, that it is hardly ever noted. But it is a form that required practice, that had a tradition, and that carried within it some strong implications about political authority in North America. To appreciate that form and to discern Hamilton's and Madison's understanding of it will be the effort of this book.

The best way to begin is by reexamining other approaches to the *Federalist*. Traditions die hard. But to see these essays on their own terms we must question and, in part, set aside some misleading notions: that they express Hamilton's or Madison's personal ideology, that they echo the main ideas of a rigorous philosophy, or that they fully represent or anticipate the aspirations of other patriots. This work has to be done tactfully, for we shall see that some roots of truth are entangled with these persistent legends. And the legends themselves demonstrate an abiding and legitimate reverence for these papers.

The *Federalist* and Ratification

The easiest misconception to attack is that the *Federalist* papers directly influenced ratification of the Constitution. At first glance, this seems to be what they were designed to do—reach a wide public in New York and elsewhere with persuasive reasons in favor of a positive vote. But the process of ratification was much more complex than this view allows. The *Federalist* did not reach very far or achieve enormous popularity throughout America, and there were more powerful forces that swayed the final voting, especially in New York.

Ratification took place not by direct vote, but through special conventions called in each state. In New York there was a long delay. The Constitution was submitted to the states by Congress in late September 1787. But the New York Legislature did not meet until the next January, and it did not develop plans for the state convention until the end of that month. Delegates were elected in April, they met in June, they came to a final vote on July 25. The *Federalist* papers meanwhile ran from October 27 until early April. The collected papers appeared in two volumes on March 22 and May 28, and the last eight installments continued to run in the newspapers from June into August. Thus, the arguments in the *Federalist* ran parallel to the New York campaign over ratification, but they did not address it directly.

Since most of the papers appeared first in several New York newspapers, they did constitute a steady campaign of ideas. A few thousand copies found several thousand readers in New York City. But beyond that confined area they were not widely published. Communications were slow and irregular. A few individual numbers of the *Federalist* were reprinted as far away as Virginia. Papers 2–19 came out weekly in the *Pennsylvania Gazette*; seven early numbers were reprinted in Boston; a dozen or so reappeared in newspapers of upstate New York. Elsewhere these writings were eclipsed by the essays of local authors. Besides, it is impossible to know how many voters could read, or would read with concentrated attention, even if these papers did come into their hands. Hamilton discussed this problem in the New York Assembly in 1787 and estimated that one-third or one-half of the men in some districts of that state were "unlettered." More recent studies suggest that New York literacy rates at this time may have run well above 70 percent for white male adults.[1] And of course even a few hundred copies in steady circulation would have reached into political conversations and touched the ears if not the eyes of many hundreds of voters. But the *Federalist* is not easy to read or to hear. Anyone who tries

---

[1] Elaine F. Crane, "Publius in the Provinces: Where Was *The Federalist* Reprinted outside New York City," *William and Mary Quarterly*, 3d ser., 21 (1964), 589–592; Linda Grant De Pauw, *The Eleventh Pillar: New York State and the Federal Constitution* (Ithaca, N.Y., 1966), pp. 109–111; *The Papers of Alexander Hamilton*, ed. Harold C. Syrett and Jacob E. Cooke, 24 vols. (New York, 1961–1979), IV, 31 (hereafter cited as *PAH*); Kenneth A. Lockridge, *Literacy in Colonial New England* (New York, 1974), pp. 74, 114; Lawrence A. Cremin, *American Education: The Colonial Experience, 1607–1783* (New York, 1970), p. 546.

to quote aloud and at length from one of the papers will soon see that they demand very attentive study.

Even where they were read these papers were not necessarily welcomed. Some readers registered a stony dislike. "Twenty-seven Subscribers" wrote to the publisher of the *New-York Journal* in late December, complaining that the series was "become nauseous" by appearing in four of the five New York newspapers. Perhaps they were half in jest, for their letter seems designed to entertain fellow readers; but the publisher complied by dropping the series a few weeks later.[2] Antifederalist writers naturally found little to commend, and some of their attacks emphasized that the *Federalist* was hard to digest. "The dry trash of Publius in 150 numbers" someone called it in May, dismissing in a phrase the demanding arguments and the extraordinary length to which they had run.[3] More disinterested was the report to France from the chargé in New York. In a description of political leaders in 1788, he mentioned the *Federalist* as an example of Hamilton's lofty but ineffective rhetoric. "That work is of no use to the well-informed, and it is too learned and too long for the ignorant."[4]

With such confined circulation and limited appeal, the *Federalist* could hardly rival other major forces in the ratification contests. The personalities of candidates for the conventions were often well known. In New York, the federalists were led by such men as Hamilton and John Jay, whose names were well established; the opposition was headed by the governor, George Clinton. Slates of candi-

---

[2] *New-York Journal*, January 1, 1788; the letter is set off in italic type and begins with a jocular remark.

[3] *New-York Journal*, May 16, 1788.

[4] Louis G. Otto, quoted in Max Farrand, ed., *The Records of the Federal Convention of 1787*, rev. ed., 4 vols. (New Haven, 1937), III, 234. This passage is cited along with other contemporary criticisms in De Pauw, *Eleventh Pillar*, pp. 114–117.

dates on both sides were well circulated among the voters, who likely saw and heard many of them in person. New York's geographical position between New England and the mid-Atlantic states also made it a conspicuous battleground for several constitutional issues, including state and federal jurisdiction over interstate commerce. New York City had been the seat of the American Congress in recent years; many city dwellers had a special interest in retaining and expanding federal offices there. On a larger scale, the Constitution carried its own authority, both in its solution of problems that had called for remedy beyond the Articles of Confederation and in its sanction by the signers, including George Washington and famous delegates from every region. Madison wrote privately that if the Constitution had been "framed & recommended by an obscure individual, instead of a body possessing public respect & confidence, there can not be a doubt, that altho' it would have stood in the identical words, it would have commanded little attention from most of those who now admire its wisdom. . . . I infer from these considerations that if a Government be ever adopted in America, it must result from a fortunate coincidence of leading opinions, and a general confidence of the people in those who may recommend it."[5] And in the end, the long delay in ratification put New York in an anomalous situation. When nine states had ratified, the Constitution came into force. When Virginia became the tenth, New York's refusal would make that state an odd outsider, surrounded by a strong new federal system. All these pressures had more actual effect on voters and members of the state convention than did any series of essays in the newspapers.

[5] *The Papers of James Madison*, ed. Robert A. Rutland et al., x (Chicago, 1977), 355–356 (hereafter cited as *PJM*).

Such essays did help sharpen these debates and lent strength of conviction to state delegates who favored the Constitution. The collected edition of the *Federalist* was rushed from the press to Virginia, presumably to serve as debater's handbook for the convention there.[6] Still, second-hand influence is a dubious distinction, and the strategy could backfire. Who wants to hear a recital of ideas he would rather not read? George Clinton simply stopped listening to Hamilton in the debates at Poughkeepsie and used the time to write a letter: "I steal this Moment while . . . the little Great Man [is] employed in repeating over Parts of Publius to us, to drop you a line."[7]

Altogether the facts of the situation do not allow the *Federalist* a very large or potent role in the actual decision making of 1787–1788. Its authors no doubt intended these papers to reach as widely as they could and to affect public opinion as much as possible. But that is a different aim. In terms of affecting votes or justifying the outcome in any state convention, the *Federalist* was in fact very marginal.

The Views of Hamilton and Madison

A more enduring claim is that Hamilton and Madison have here set down their leading ideas about government in America. Even if they were not heeded when they first appeared, these essays contain the considered views of two of the architects of the Constitution, who soon became its leading interpreters. This idea has persisted for two centuries and still holds sway. Biographies and selected writ-

[6] Hamilton to Madison, May 11 and 18, 1788, in *PAH*, IV, 648, 650.
[7] George Clinton to John Lamb, June 1788, cited by De Pauw (*Eleventh Pillar*, p. 210), who has caught a similar gibe in the remarks of Melancton Smith (p. 199).

ings of both men depend so heavily on these papers that
their political characters are now understood in light of
what they wrote here. But this view of the *Federalist* is also
difficult to sustain.

Neither Hamilton nor Madison, in the first place, could
write wholeheartedly in support of the proposed constitution. Their private papers make this clear. Neither believed
that the compromises worked out in Philadelphia would
suffice for a strong government. Their essays in the *Federalist* are the best defense they could make of a new constitution that seemed better than the old confederation. The
essays are to that extent forced and do not represent the
authors' personal, considered thoughts about American
politics.

"No man's ideas were more remote from the plan than
his were known to be," Hamilton told the Convention on
the day of the signing. When he alone signed for New
York, he was deciding "between anarchy and Convulsion
on one side, and the chance of good to be expected from
the plan, on the other" (*PAH*, IV, 253). A few days later he
wrote out "Conjectures about the New Constitution," a
memorandum of his private thoughts which records the
same doubt. If the Constitution were not adopted, he imagined that there might be an upheaval among the states,
even a civil war. If it were adopted, the best hope lay in
gradual revision of the federal organization which would
"perhaps enable the government to acquire more consistency than the proposed constitution seems to promise"
(*PAH*, IV, 276).

Madison was just as pessimistic. To most of his correspondents he must have seemed sanguine and energetic,
catching every opportunity to further the ratification campaign. But to Thomas Jefferson—who was then in Paris as
minister to France—he showed a different mood. At the

close of the Convention he wrote "that the plan should it be adopted will neither effectually answer its national object nor prevent the local mischiefs which every where excite disgusts against the state governments" (*PJM*, x, 163–164). In a long letter of October 24, he explained that the faults were radical. At the Convention he had proposed a veto power that the national government would hold over state legislation as a way of keeping local tyrannies in check. This proposal had been narrowly rejected, but its defeat left Madison in despair. This letter contains an "immoderate digression" on the importance of this veto power. Without it, there would be no final arbiter in disputes between states and the federal government. And within states there would be no escape from unstable government and oppression over minorities.[8]

These are severe criticisms, evidence of deep misgivings. But of course there is no hint of such doubts in the pages of the *Federalist*. Did Hamilton and Madison change their minds? Their later behavior does not show it. Hamilton is notorious for his loose construction of the Constitution, as a way to enlarge federal powers. And Madison was willing to modify the Constitution with amendments as soon as he came into Congress. Certainly both men supported the Constitution as it was proposed to the voters. But the *Federalist* essays catch them in a false position, supporting it absolutely and so reasoning against their own deepest convictions.

These authors also kept themselves distant from this project, both while it was in press and long afterward. They kept its authorship hidden from some of their closest

---

[8]*PJM*, x, 209–214. For a full account of Madison's position on the federal veto power, see Charles F. Hobson, "The Negative on State Laws: James Madison, the Constitution, and the Crisis of Republican Government," *William and Mary Quarterly*, 3d ser., 36 (1979), 215–235.

friends, and promoted its influence very obliquely. Much of this caution can be explained as ordinary political prudence. The *Federalist* came out over a pseudonym. Both Hamilton and Madison were known; they might be embarrassed or rendered ineffective if they were exposed in collaboration; and personal letters could not be trusted for such confidential matters. Hamilton sent copies of the published *Federalist* essays to Benjamin Rush in November and encouraged him to have them reprinted in Philadelphia, but he touched on authorship very lightly: "They are going on and appear evidently to be written by different hands and to aim at a full examination of the subject" (*PAH*, iv, 333). Madison was equally cautious in urging reprintings through the efforts of Washington, John Randolph, and Tench Coxe.[9] Any hint of authorial pride was swept away by disclaimers that the series was obviously the disjointed labor of several hands.

It is curious, however, that Madison also kept this secret from Jefferson. We have already seen that he wrote out a lengthy critique of the Constitution for this friend. Yet he was silent about these published essays as their correspondence continued. Almost a year went by, and it was not until the entire series was published and ratification was accomplished—not until August, 1788—that he revealed his hand in the project. Even then he was forced into it, and he urged Jefferson to secrecy by writing in cipher. "Col. Carrington tells me he has sent you the first volume of the federalist, and adds the 2d. by this conveyance. I believe I never have yet mentioned to you that publication. It was undertaken last fall by Jay, Hamilton and myself. The proposal came from the two former. The

---

[9] *PJM*, x, 254, 290, 445. To Archibald Stuart's warm praise of the essays Madison returned a curt reply; see *PJM*, x, 245, 271.

execution was thrown by the sickness of Jay mostly on the two others. Though carried on in concert the writers are not mutually answerable for all the ideas of each other, there being seldom time for even a perusal of the pieces by any but the writer before they were wanted at the press and some times hardly by the writer himself."[10] This is very casual or matter of fact, if not apologetic, concerning a series that is said to contain the kernel of Madison's thought. And Madison remained dismissive. His next letter to Jefferson contains a long discussion of whether or not the Constitution should contain a bill of rights, but it has not one word about *Federalist* No. 84, which covers the same ground (*PTJ*, XIV, 18–21).

As years went by, both Hamilton and Madison remained generally indifferent toward this work. They had good reasons as active politicians, and later as political enemies, for keeping their authorship secret. But once that secret came into the open, and new editions were promoted, they remained aloof and dismissive. There is a romantic tale to the effect that Hamilton, on the eve of his duel with Aaron Burr, slipped a note into the books of an old friend so as to leave for posterity a final record of which *Federalist* papers he had written. But this note has not been seen since 1818 and that it existed at all is very doubtful.[11] Hamilton took a hand more directly in the 1802 edition, published by George F. Hopkins. Hopkins explained the procedure decades later to Hamilton's son: "Your father, it appeared, did not regard the work with much partiality; but, nevertheless, consented to republication on condition that it should

---

[10] Madison to Jefferson, August 10, 1788, in *The Papers of Thomas Jefferson*, ed. Julian P. Boyd, XIII (Princeton, 1956), 498–499.

[11] *The Federalist*, ed. Jacob E. Cooke (Middletown, Conn., 1961), pp. xxi–xxiii. All references to the *Federalist* are to this edition unless otherwise noted.

undergo a careful revision." The revisions were largely stylistic; according to Hopkins they were made by one of the "respectable professional gentlemen" who first proposed the edition, then reviewed by Hamilton himself. But Hamilton refused to disclose exactly who wrote which papers. He thus held at arm's length the only later edition to which he gave any attention. Hopkins concludes that Hamilton distinctly preferred some of his other writings. "The letters of Pacificus [1793] were added at your father's suggestion; and corrected with his own hand. He remarked to me at the time; that 'some of his friends had pronounced them to be his best performance.'"[12]

In 1818 another publisher offered Madison the chance to supply a list of attributions. The resulting Gideon edition proclaimed itself as the final, perfect text. "The publisher of this volume has been so fortunate as to procure from Mr. Madison the copy of the work which that gentleman had preserved for himself, with corrections of the papers, of which he is the author, in his own hand."[13] But these corrections were minor. Madison, like Hamilton, refrained from recasting any essays or publishing any later thoughts on their contents. Seeing that Hamilton had appended the "Pacificus" papers, he merely agreed to add his own "Helvidius" papers, which had been written in reply to them. Some time later Madison wrote out a rather long memorandum concerning the *Federalist* and its editions. He recorded details about how the series began and why the papers were disjointed. As in the letter to Jefferson, he complained about the pressures of a tight schedule. He could hardly have written what he did without the aid of his notes from the Convention and "familiarity with the

---

[12] George F. Hopkins to John C. Hamilton, February 4, 1847, in *The Federalist*, ed. John C. Hamilton (Philadelphia, 1864), I, xci–xcii.
[13] Quoted in *The Federalist*, ed. Cooke, p. xvii.

whole subject produced by the discussions there. It frequently happened that whilst the printer was putting into type the parts of a number, the following parts were under the pen, & to be furnished in time for the press." Madison also recorded a few lines about editorial policy.

> In the beginning it was the practice of the writers, of A. H. & J. M. particularly to communicate each to the other, their respective papers before they were sent to the press. This was rendered so inconvenient, by the shortness of the time allowed, that it was dispensed with. Another reason was, that it was found most agreeable to each, not to give a positive sanction to all the doctrines and sentiments of the other; there being a known difference in the general complexion of their political theories.[14]

It is hard to know what to make of this. Papers were sometimes produced in haste; the preface to the 1788 edition, by Hamilton, seems to agree on that point: "The particular circumstances under which these papers have been written, have rendered it impractical to avoid violations of method and repetitions of ideas which cannot but displease a critical reader."[15] But it is not so clear that Hamilton and Madison knew themselves to be uneasily allied. Madison is here writing more than thirty years after the fact, thirty years full of great public events in which he regularly found himself opposed to Hamilton and his party. And this passage admits that at the beginning the two main authors did consult and sanction each other's work.[16] What does

---

[14] Elizabeth Fleet, ed., "Madison's 'Detatched Memoranda,'" *William and Mary Quarterly*, 3d ser., 3 (1946), 565.

[15] Quoted in *The Federalist*, ed. J. C. Hamilton, I, lxxxviii.

[16] Two further, detailed problems also arise. First, Madison says it was the practice of Hamilton and Madison "particularly" to read each

come out clearly is that Madison continued to feel uneasy about the *Federalist*. He may have asserted his claims to authorship, and basked in some resulting celebrity and authority, but the work as a whole never seemed properly finished or consistent, or quite worthy of the fame it had attained.

Both Hamilton and Madison, then, held themselves in when looking back on this series. It was not what either of them would have made it. The parts each one claimed were mingled with writings he could no longer support. Subsequent decades have also demonstrated that it would be impossible to disentangle them. Hamilton's and Madison's editors have tried every means of testing their conflicting claims to some papers, but only to reveal how closely allied these writers were in this particular case.

External evidence (the Gideon edition and private lists made by both authors) results in conflicting claims over thirteen of the eighty-five papers. But internal evidence cannot resolve this problem. Avowed Hamiltonians have found parallel passages in that New Yorker's other writings, which persuade them of his authorship. But avowed

---

other's papers. Does this mean "in particular," that is, as opposed to other collaborators? That would be strange, because the only other writer was Jay; he had contributed all but one of his essays before Madison's first contribution appeared and that one (No. 64) appeared months later. Then does the word "particularly" mean "scrupulously," and if so does it imply that Madison and Hamilton worked in very close collaboration? Second, Madison says that this practice was abandoned. If so, when? Madison claimed to have written Nos. 10, 14, 18, 19, and 20 before beginning a run of twenty-two essays (Nos. 37–58), then contributing briefly (Nos. 62 and 63) before leaving the project completely and returning to Virginia. The "practice" can hardly have deserved that name if it did not extend through No. 20; it cannot have been "dispensed with" by Madison's departure after No. 63. But if there had emerged a clear distrust between the two collaborators would Hamilton have allowed Madison free reign over the next twenty-two installments? And would Madison have continued, knowing that Hamilton might veer into distasteful doctrines in his remaining portion?

Madisonians have found line-by-line parallels just as convincing in the collected works of their hero.[17] A scrupulous modern editor can only throw up his hands, summarize this evidence, and come to an ambiguous conclusion: "If one were to rely on internal evidence, it . . . would be impossible to assign all the disputed essays to either Hamilton or Madison" (*The Federalist*, ed. Cooke, p. xxix). Modern editions of both men's papers continue to segregate their *Federalist* essays, but only after elaborate and despairing reviews of the whole protracted controversy.

An attempt has even been made to apply modern science to the problem. All the papers have been subjected to computer analysis—with results that nicely reinforce one author's claims. But the history of that effort is another lesson in ambiguity. The statisticians who undertook the task labored through several stages—and two decades—to find a definite, perceptible difference in these writers' styles. Sentence length proved a failure (Hamilton's average sentence in the *Federalist* contains 34.55 words; Madison's, 34.59). Marker words, unique to either writer, could not be found in sufficient numbers to identify the disputed passages. Trivial, unobtrusive words were finally screened and their frequencies of use by both authors were tabulated to make up statistical profiles. But this was a way of mea-

---

[17] Hamiltonians include John C. Hamilton, Henry Cabot Lodge (who edited Hamilton's *Works* in 1886), and Paul Leicester Ford, who replied to Edward Bourne in the same volume of the *American Historical Review* cited below. Madisonians include Edward G. Bourne, "The Authorship of the Federalist," *American Historical Review*, 2 (1896–1897), 443–460, 682–687; Douglass Adair, "The Authorship of the Disputed Federalist Papers," *William and Mary Quarterly*, 3d ser., 1 (1944), 97–122, 235–264 (rpt. in Douglass Adair, *Fame and the Founding Fathers*, ed. Trevor Colbourn [New York, 1974], pp. 27–74). Other scholars, without taking sides, have tacitly assumed a sharp distinction between the two authors' contributions. Typical is Alpheus T. Mason, "The Federalist—A Split Personality," *American Historical Review*, 57 (1957), 625–643.

suring differences which only a computer could sort out. The result was expressed in probabilities, all in favor of Madison. But the entire process shows that the two authors really cannot be distinguished by any reader who looks directly at their vocabulary, style, or ideas.[18]

Thus it is difficult to see how the *Federalist* or any part of it can be used as a fair sample of Hamilton's or Madison's way of thinking. Each of them wrote contrary to his convictions, avoided revealing his hand, expressed his dissatisfaction about the work as a whole, and contributed a share that merged indistinguishably with writings he would later disclaim. Disguise, silence, distance, and disavowal do not add up to warm authorial approval. Consistencies between sections of these papers and portions of either man's other writings do not prove that these are typical, let alone specially canonical. What they indicate instead is that this work is special, that it represents a temporary, strong, and intricate collaboration—one that drew upon strengths from both partners but altered and sometimes compounded them to suit the needs of a unique public debate.

The Ideas of the Founders

A third view of the *Federalist* is that it represents the thinking not of Hamilton or of Madison alone, but of the Founders generally who framed and ratified the Constitution. This idea rests on some loose associations, of course, but it

[18] Frederick Mosteller and David L. Wallace, *Inference and Disputed Authorship: The Federalist* (Reading, Mass., 1964). A more accessible account is Ivor S. Francis, "An Exposition of a Statistical Approach to the Federalist Dispute," in *The Computer and Literary Style*, ed. Jacob Leed (Kent, Ohio, 1966), pp. 38–77.

contains enough truth to make it very appealing. Hamilton may not have agreed with everything he wrote here, but he was the lone delegate from New York to sign at the Convention. The *Federalist* was his energetic effort to promote the Constitution in his home state. Madison may not have been entirely optimistic, but he too lent a hand. As he said later, he could not have written so well except that he was saturated in the Convention debates, which he had assiduously recorded. Together the alliance of these two minds seems symbolic of a general persuasion among political leaders. They swallowed their private disappointments over some details of the Constitution and worked hard to achieve its acceptance. The *Federalist* may not have influenced the outcome of the state conventions. But it endured as the most widely accepted argument in favor of ratification, and it earned the praise of many early patriots. The deepest problem with this view is that it comes close to confusing the *Federalist* with the Constitution itself. Those who accept it also risk identifying both documents as hazy symbols of an ideal intellectual consensus. We have now seen that the *Federalist* could bore some readers and irritate others, just as the proposed Constitution could provoke some very sensible patriots to passionate outrage. What those opponents saw clearly has not vanished because they lost and acquiesced. The Constitution would make sweeping changes in American government. The force of those changes would depend on how particular clauses were interpreted. And the *Federalist* purported to explain the limited possibilities of interpretation. We have also seen that this explanation did not satisfy either of the principal authors. Once ratification was complete, Hamilton went one way in abandoning views expounded in the *Federalist* and Madison went another. This was no trivial

difference. Federalists and Republicans could hardly be held from strife during the presidency of Washington, and their mutual suspicions of treason grew worse thereafter. The Constitution endured because it commanded deeper loyalties than either party and because it could grow and develop to meet new circumstances. But that was not true of the *Federalist*.

No one understood this difference better than James Madison, who had many occasions for publicly commenting on the Founders' intentions. Early and late he saw that the *Federalist* could be used not only as a touchstone of ideas but also as a stinging political weapon. He used it that way himself. When he wrote the "Helvidius" papers in 1793, in reply to Hamilton's "Pacificus," he made long quotations from *Federalist* No. 72 by Hamilton, which ran directly against the policy "Pacificus" was supporting. Madison also made the most of his authority, introducing the *Federalist* passages as "an extract from a work which entered into a systematic explanation and defense of the constitution; and to which there has frequently been ascribed some influence in conciliating the public assent to the government in the form proposed."[19] But he found this form of argument dreary and he gave it up very quickly. He no doubt recognized that if Hamilton could be embarrassed by the *Federalist* so could Madison. In fact his authorship was to haunt him throughout his public career, and betray him at the end of it. At the Virginia state constitutional convention in 1829 he argued in favor of white male suffrage, only to be reminded of the different policy he had favored in *Federalist* No. 54. An opposition orator

---

[19] *Helvidius*, No. 1, in Marvin Meyers, ed., *The Mind of the Founder: Sources of the Political Thought of James Madison* (Indianapolis, 1973), p. 272.

caught Madison with such an odd facial expression that it brought down the house in convulsive laughter.[20]

As Madison grew old he survived all the other Founding Fathers and became the living curator of the ideas that had gone into the Constitution. It was known that he had been a leading member of the Convention, that he had recorded the Philadelphia debates and carefully preserved them, that he had written much of the *Federalist*, and that he had been an effective force in every early administration. He remained active into his eighties, and it is astonishing to discover him writing to those great senatorial debaters, Robert Hayne and Daniel Webster—and setting them straight about what the Union meant—more than fifty-five years after he first held public office. His extraordinary personal authority in old age may have merged the Convention, the Constitution, and the *Federalist* in one place in his countrymen's memories.

But his own mind held all these things lucidly apart. He never hinted, for example, that the *Federalist* was in any way a direct digest of the leading ideas he had recorded in Philadelphia. Nor did he feel that either those essays or those recorded debates could fairly represent the meaning of the Constitution. To the end of his life he refused to publish the debates, and he explained why. "In general it had appeared to me," he wrote in 1821, "that it might be best to let the work be a posthumous one; or at least that its publication should be delayed till the Constitution should be well settled by practice, & till a knowledge of the controversial part of the proceedings of its framers could be turned to no improper account. Delicacy also seemed to

[20] Irving Brant, *James Madison: Commander in Chief 1812–1836* (Indianapolis, 1961), p. 464.

[35]

require some respect to the rule by which the Convention 'prohibited a promulgation without leave of what was spoken in it;' so long as the policy of that rule could be regarded as in any degree unexpired." In other words, Madison still held a deep scruple about the confidentiality of the debates. Though he does not say it, that scruple must have been heavy on his shoulders when he was conspicuously taking notes in 1787 and later when he was preparing *Federalist* essays for publication. Moreover, he goes on here, the debates may seem to have an authority they utterly lack.

> As a guide in expounding and applying the provisions of the Constitution, the debates and incidental decisions of the Convention can have no authoritative character. However desirable it be that they should be preserved as a gratification to the laudable curiosity felt by every people to trace the origin and progress of the political Institutions, & as a source perhaps of some lights on the Science of Govt. the legitimate meaning of the Instrument must be derived from the text itself; or if a key is to be sought elsewhere, it must be not in the opinions or intentions of the Body which planned & proposed the Constitution, but in the sense attached to it by the people in their respective State Conventions where it recd. all the authority which it possesses.[21]

This is rigorous constitutionalism. The opportunity is wide open here for a word about the *Federalist* or the authority of the Convention, but both are rejected in favor of the text itself. If further clarity is needed, one should look not

[21] Madison to Thomas Ritchie, September 15, 1821, in Farrand, *Records*, III, 447–448.

to the intentions of the authors, but to the understanding of the electorate. The last sentence closely echoes the theory of the Tenth Amendment: "The powers not delegated to the United States by the Constitution, nor prohibited by it to the States, are reserved to the States respectively, or to the people."

Even when he was pressed by his closest ally, Madison did not swerve. Jefferson's last great cause was the founding of the University of Virginia, and in 1825 he was concerned about the studies in the law school there. He sent Madison a proposed resolve of the Board of Visitors, which in its final form declared that "the best guides" to general principles of government in America were to be found in a definite list of texts. Heading the list were "1. the Declaration of Independence, as the fundamental act of union of these states. 2. the book known by the title of 'The Federalist,' being an authority to which appeal is habitually made by all, and rarely declined or denied by any as evidence of the general opinion of those who framed, and of those who accepted the Constitution of the US. on questions as to it's genuine meaning." [22] This is fulsome, flattering, and tempting, not least because it places Madison's most famous writing right next to Jefferson's. But Madison saw the entire proposal for what it was, a move to close off freedom of learning by the prescription of orthodox texts, many of them colored with the ideals of the Republican party. He would not cross Jefferson concerning his university; he did not oppose the resolve. But he wrote

[22] Minutes of the Board of Visitors of the University of Virginia, March 4, 1825. I quote from the scrupulous transcription of documents which is appended to a cogent modern defense of Jefferson's plan; see Arthur Bestor, "Thomas Jefferson and the Freedom of Books," in Arthur Bestor, David C. Mearns, and Jonathan Daniels, *Three Presidents and Their Books* (Urbana, Ill., 1955), p. 43.

back a careful critique of every item on the list. The Declaration, he remarked quietly, "tho' rich in fundamental principles, and saying everything that could be said in the same number of words," could still offer no safeguards for *interpreting* a constitution. It could "afford no aid in guarding our Republican Charters against constructive violations." Concerning the *Federalist*, Madison also seems to agree with Jefferson's judgment, but then very tactfully qualifies it:

> The 'Federalist' may fairly enough be regarded as the most authentic exposition of the text of the federal Constitution, as understood by the Body which prepared & the authorities which accepted it. Yet it did not foresee all the misconstructions which have occurred; nor prevent some that it did foresee. And what equally deserves remark, neither of the great rival parties have acquiesced in all its comments. It may nevertheless be admissible as a School book, if any will be that goes so much into detail. It has been actually admitted into two Universities, if not more, those of Harvard & Rh[ode] Island; but probably at the choice of the Professors, without an injunction from the superior authority.[23]

If we read this through Madison's eyes rather than Jefferson's, every phrase strains with ambiguities and reservations: Maybe the *Federalist* is the best surviving public argument from the time of ratification, but it is vulnerable to misinterpretation. Neither Hamilton's party nor ours could ever completely endorse it. It may introduce beginning students to problems that we have found more intri-

[23] Madison to Jefferson, February 8, 1825, in Bestor, *Three Presidents*, p. 41.

cate by experience, but it is cumbersome even for that purpose. When assigned in a university it deserves questioning rather than forced acceptance. Gently but firmly, Madison undermines whatever praise he allows and puts the *Federalist* in its place—far lower than the pinnacle of true constitutional authority.

A Rigorous Political Theory

The last exaggerated claim about the *Federalist* is that it contains a rigorous political philosophy. According to this view, these papers generally address the issues of their time, but within them, or within parts of them, there are nuggets of theoretical understanding which raise Hamilton and Madison to eminence among the great thinkers of the world. They have been set against Plato, Aristotle, Machiavelli, Montesquieu, Hume, the moral sense philosophers of the Scottish Enlightenment, Kant, and Marx, among others. Perhaps the most influential discussion of this sort has been Charles Beard's *An Economic Interpretation of the Constitution of the United States* (1913), which found principles of economic determinism in the phrases of *Federalist* No. 10. But an impulse to find an elaborate framework of principles in the *Federalist* can be seen in panegyrics as well as in critiques, and from the time of its publication down to the present.

This view is understandably tempting; it is also impossible to refute. The *Federalist* is not an easy polemical pamphlet. It makes a display of learning and seems to derive many of its conclusions from high axioms of government. A modern reader also comes to its pages knowing that they were written by studious, principled men. Hamilton had a steady brilliance to match his ambition, and if Madison was not exactly a political scholar he was a prodigy among his contemporaries for a ready command of bookish learning. In the *Federalist*, if anywhere, one might look for the amplest application of intellect to the foundations of American institutions. Furthermore, the fact that it deals with "axioms" and principles at all automatically lifts it into the realm of philosophy. Whether the authors intended it or not, these essays ask for comparison with the most celebrated works of political theory.

But if such comparisons have to be made, they must be made with caution. For "philosophy" can be a slippery term, sometimes a purely honorific one. If it means that the *Federalist* draws deductions from arguable premises, and takes account of a great body of learning, no one can deny the term's appropriateness. If it means that the *Federalist* contains an ideology—a general framework of values and principles behind a political persuasion—it is still a useful term. It is defensible even if it means that a specific ideology or combination of political ideals is developed within these pages. But should it imply that the *Federalist* expounds a systematic way of thinking about life, that it provides a doctrine which can be taught and elaborated, that it contains far-reaching reflections on the universe and man's place within it?

The latter view may seem manifestly absurd, except that it emerges explicitly in many approaches to this work. Beard, for example, falls into very extravagant language. "*The Federalist* presents the political science of the new system as conceived by three of the profoundest thinkers of the period." Later on the same page he writes that it "is in fact the finest study in the economic interpretation of politics which exists in any language." And three pages later: "The most philosophical examination of the foundations of political science is made by Madison in the tenth number."[24] Does he mean "profoundest thinkers" in comparison with other American statesmen or in comparison with all men of the eighteenth century? When he says "most philosophical" does he mean in relation to other *Federalist* arguments or absolutely? Since Beard does not make his meaning clear he leaves the impression that the *Federalist* marks a turning point in the history of Western thought. Just as misleading have been more recent attempts to link Hamilton and Madison directly to the great philosophers of their time. Douglass Adair has very sharply discussed the meanings and overtones of the word "philosophy," but only to insist that Madison was a true philosopher. He calls him "the most creative and philosophical disciple of the Scottish school of science and politics in the Philadelphia Convention." Adair makes this judgment after tracing close verbal parallels between *Federalist* No. 10 and several political essays by David Hume. He concludes that Madison carried "glad news" to Philadelphia. "This was the message he gave to the world in the first *Federalist* paper he composed. His own scientific reading of history, ancient and modern, his experience with religious factions in Virginia, and above all his knowledge of the scientific axiom regarding man and society in the works of David Hume, ablest British philosopher of his age, had served him and his country well."[25] Madison was not only a philosopher, but a figure who made momentous improvements on the most penetrating philosophy of his time.

Without going into the intricacies of Beard's and Adair's

---

[24] Charles A. Beard, *An Economic Interpretation of the Constitution of the United States* (1913, 1935; rpt. New York, 1965), pp. 153, 156.

[25] Douglass Adair, "'That Politics May Be Reduced to a Science': David Hume, James Madison, and the Tenth Federalist," *Huntington Library Quarterly*, 20 (1957), 343-360 (rpt. in Adair, *Fame*, pp. 93-106).

arguments right now, we can see that they evolve from very tortuous analysis and from some assumptions we have already questioned. These scholars select single papers or isolated passages, without regard to the consistency of the *Federalist* as a whole. They ascribe these passages to a single author, imputing to him a certain range of reading, study, or political outlook. They then match the passage and the imputed background to reveal a depth of philosophy not only in the *Federalist* but also in the Philadelphia Convention and in the Constitution. Beard, who had misgivings about the Constitution, identifies Madison as a force shaping its economic conservatism. Adair, who revered the Constitution, exalts Madison as its intellectual hero. But if Madison's personal beliefs cannot be surely distinguished in these papers, even from Hamilton's, it is hard to contend that parallel passages from Hume or anyone else can be traced through Madison's mind and directly into the wording of any passage. And if the *Federalist* cannot be cited as an exact account of the Founders' intentions, then a "profound philosophy" in these papers has only a tenuous relevance to the Constitution.

And at this point we can see a further reason for questioning such discussions of the *Federalist*. They can lead to the red-white-and-blue conclusion that the Constitution rests on a coherent, explicit, rigid system of ideas. Scholars may differ about whether this philosophy is to be located finally in the Constitution, the *Federalist* (or a part of it), the mind of Madison, the works of Hume, or the nature of mankind. But this way of reasoning discloses that such a creed exists, that it is expounded in the *Federalist*, and that it can stand up against any other system of thought. In later chapters we shall see that such a notion is actually repugnant to the *Federalist*, and particularly to No. 10. But, to put it mildly for now, it is a notion of such patriotic glow as to subvert disinterested historical research by an American scholar.

It is evident, too, that Madison, Hamilton, and Jay—and for that matter John Adams, Jefferson, John Dickinson, and a half dozen other early controversialists—never thought of themselves as great systematic philosophers. None of them worked out a formal philosophical treatise; all of them devoted their public writings to policy issues as they emerged, year in and year out; and any one of them, in his prime, might have sat down after dinner any day of the week and penned a dozen closely reasoned pages on a current issue, in very shrewd language and drawing upon large reserves of learning, historical and legal. Scholarly statesmen, yes; far-reaching philosophers, no. There is a difference. When ratification was over Madison and Hamilton both turned away from their arguments in the *Federalist* and reverted to them again only when public events made it necessary. They did not refine, reconsider, debate, or consolidate them further. In large measure they set them aside. They had more immediate challenges to attend to.

Having surveyed these ways of approaching the *Federalist*—as a decisive case for ratification, a manifesto of either Hamilton or Madison, an orthodox reading of the Constitution, and a work of high philosophy—we can note one feature common to all of them: they regard this work mainly as a finished book. They look back at it as a bound volume that emerged from the welter of ephemeral debates, one that has endured in a fame reinforced by the long history of the Constitution. They raise expectations that its pages contain a definitive statement about American life. In fact, they suggest that this book is to be held in awe rather than critically studied.

To see the *Federalist* on its own terms, however, means

to begin anew—to go back through the musty files of old newspapers, trace the haphazard growth of a doubtful and tentative project, and observe the development of consistency in a very unlikely collaboration. This review of a serial-in-progress will yield two important results. First, it will show that there are good grounds for the authority of the *Federalist*. Indeed, we will be able to qualify and refine older approaches and survey the full outline of a very thoughtful case for federal, constitutional government. Second, this review will cast new light on the importance of Hamilton and Madison's authorship. We will see that their strengths lie not so much in their theoretical ideas, or in what they seem to say on any particular page, as in their imaginative grasp of how to address an American public on this unique occasion for political discussion.

CHAPTER TWO

The Form of the *Federalist*

To understand the design of the *Federalist*, one has to look not only at its first appearances in New York newspapers, but also at the backgrounds from which it emerged. Seen in retrospect, or in isolation, it seems an astonishing work of political argument, quite distinctive from other, briefer, or more scattered publications of its time. But in fact these papers developed toward such distinction. Their fundamental plan rested on a canny appraisal of rival essay series and a shrewd and fortuitous handling of tone, publication, and collaboration. What grew from these resources was a series of papers knit together by a special strategy of discourse—the polite, thorough reasoning of a figure named Publius, who came forward with an informed overview of national government and an assured sense of how to address all challengers.

Hamilton's Rivals and Resources

The idea for the *Federalist* came from Alexander Hamilton. There is a family legend that he wrote the first paper while traveling on the Hudson River by sloop in the fall of 1787.[1] But whatever its precise origins, there is no doubt that Hamilton planned the series, negotiated its publication, chose its other authors, supervised its development, wrote most of its papers, arranged its republication in book form, and drew it to a conclusion. Moreover, he did all this on his own American ground, on the island of Manhattan in the city of New York. He handled publishing resources that were familiar to him, and began a lengthy defense of the Constitution for readers to whom he was already very well known.

Before the first issue appeared Hamilton had already put himself forward concerning the Constitution. He was the lone delegate from his state to sign it, and he had returned home alert to the political climate in which it would be received. While the Philadelphia Convention was still sitting in July, he had opened hostilities by publishing a long, unsigned letter in a New York newspaper, attacking Governor George Clinton and stating nine "reflections" on the need for serious alterations in the Articles of Confederation. A few weeks later he admitted his authorship in another long letter, with more remarks about Clinton as an enemy of the Convention.[2] It has been argued that these publications were gratuitous attacks, which served only to provoke opposition.[3] But Hamilton certainly believed

[1] Linda Grant De Pauw has noted two versions of this story in *The Eleventh Pillar: New York State and the Federal Constitution* (Ithaca, N.Y., 1966), p. 106.

[2] *The Daily Advertiser*, July 21 and September 15, 1787; *The Papers of Alexander Hamilton*, ed. Harold C. Syrett and Jacob E. Cooke, 24 vols. (New York, 1961-1979), IV, 229-232, 248-253 (hereafter cited as *PAH*).

[3] De Pauw (*Eleventh Pillar*, p. 73) argues largely on the basis of disinterested comments by Louis G. Otto, the French chargé d'affaires in New York. But she has confused two quotations. On July 25, 1787, Otto wrote that Clinton was "l'ennemi le plus actif et le plus dangereux de la puissance du Congrès," and he seconded Hamilton's suspicions

that Clinton was organizing his forces against whatever the Convention might produce. The second letter defied Clinton to deny his accusation. Hamilton promised "to bring forward the sources of his information and the proofs of his charge" if such a denial were published, or to retract if Clinton persuaded him privately. Perhaps in mid-July Hamilton still had hopes of a constitution to his liking and thought to undermine opposition by pointing out Clinton's maneuvers against any proposals for change. In any case, he acted. He composed something vigorous for the newspapers—as he had often done before—and he suffered the consequences. Other newspaper writers attacked him in a way that hurt, calling him a scandal-monger, a poor political loser, an upstart who had wormed his way into General Washington's favor only to be dismissed from it. Hamilton was stung enough to ask Washington for an explicit answer to that last charge (*PAH*, IV, 249n, 252n, 280–281).

This first foray therefore was very messy. As weeks passed, Hamilton had reasons to think better of it. At the same time he had to settle his own feelings about the Convention. He had seen his own strong pleas ignored before he left the deliberations in Philadelphia on June 29. But he went back in August and September, while the other New York delegates, Abraham Yates and John Lansing, left on July 10 and refused to return. With them Hamilton had not been able to act in concert; without them he was not empowered to vote; and their departure may well have sharpened his sense that Clinton and his followers would

---

that Clinton was already a busy antagonist of federal power. Later, after ratification, Otto recalled that Hamilton once had had the courage to attack Clinton in the press "sans aucune provocation," which may mean without any prior publication on Clinton's part. See Max Farrand, ed., *The Records of the Federal Convention of 1787*, rev. ed. (New Haven, 1937), III, 63, 234.

obstruct any reform. But his own role remained a puzzle. As the lone signing delegate, he would be expected to lead the ratification campaign in New York. As the vocal opponent of Clinton, he had already shown his hand. But he was evidently facing opponents who would answer blow for blow, and his deep private misgivings about the Constitution might well betray him in a pitched battle. Governor Clinton refused to be drawn out into direct confrontation in print. Hamilton had thus set himself up to do battle with chinks in his armor, against secret hands that were eager to wound. As soon as the Constitution was published he began to prepare for the worst. "The New Constitution is as popular in this City as it is possible for any thing to be," he wrote Washington in October. "But there is no saying what turn things may take when the full flood of official influence is let loose against it. This is to be expected, for though the Governor has not publicly declared himself his particular connections and confidential friends are loud against it" (*PAH*, IV, 281).

Meanwhile the newspapers were beginning to carry further essays, which showed other forms the constitutional debate might take. Letters of "Cato" began appearing in the *New-York Journal* on September 27, on the same page with the text of the new Constitution, and they were promptly answered by two "Caesar" letters in the *Daily Advertiser*. Later readers have thought that these essays were actually written by Clinton and Hamilton. They were not. But they amplified the rancor Hamilton had already experienced and demonstrated its futility. "Cato" began by mildly urging readers to weigh the Constitution on its merits, not accept it on the authority of the Convention. "Caesar" replied immediately, intemperately, and clumsily; he admitted in his second letter that his own "blunt and ungracious reasoning" led to the truth that "the mass of the people of America . . . cannot judge with any degree of precision concerning the fitness of this New Constitution." Hardly a winning appeal to common readers! To Hamilton it must have shown how badly his cause could be blackened by the ink of fools.[4]

On October 18, a very temperate essay by "Brutus" covered the second page of the *New-York Journal*. This writer opened by appealing to the solemnity of the occasion and addressing his readers with fitting respect. "Momentous then is the question you have to determine, and you are called upon by every motive which should influence a noble and virtuous mind, to examine it well, and to make up a wise judgment" (Storing, II, 364). The essay then turned to a very long, careful argument that the Constitution would lead to the obliteration of state powers. It is not known who wrote as "Brutus," but his first paper showed he had a precise and articulate grasp of fundamental issues in the debate. His last paragraph indicated he would write again, and in fact he contributed sixteen long essays, one every week or two until the following April.

"The FŒDERALIST, No. 1" appeared on October 27 and was evidently a work of careful deliberation. This new series would rise above personal animosity and treat a worthy subject with a comprehensive view and a serious tone. Like

---

[4] "Cato" is reprinted in Herbert J. Storing, ed., *The Complete Anti-Federalist*, 7 vols. (Chicago, 1981), II, 104-125, and in Paul L. Ford, ed., *Essays on the Constitution of the United States* (1892; rpt. New York, 1970), pp. 247-278. "Caesar" is reprinted in Ford, *Essays*, pp. 283-291. Clinton's authorship of "Cato" has been most vigorously denied by De Pauw in a full appendix (*Eleventh Pillar*, pp. 283-292), but Storing still leans toward that attribution (II, 103). Jacob E. Cooke has argued against Hamilton's authorship of "Caesar" in "Alexander Hamilton's Authorship of the 'Caesar' Letters," *William and Mary Quarterly*, 3d ser., 17 (1960), 78-85. There is corroborative evidence in Frederick Mosteller and David L. Wallace, *Inference and Disputed Authorship: The Federalist* (Reading, Mass., 1964), pp. 251-252.

the other continuing series, it appeared on the second page of a regular newspaper, with a title and number, though the usual formula of address, "To the Citizens of the State of New York," was slightly altered: "To the People of the State of New York." The opening paragraph carried a lofty statement of the responsibilities now being faced by both the author and his readers.

> It has been frequently remarked, that it seems to have been reserved to the people of this country, by their conduct and example, to decide the important question, whether societies of men are really capable or not, of establishing good government from reflection and choice, or whether they are forever destined to depend, for their political constitutions, on accident and force. If there be any truth in the remark, the crisis, at which we are arrived, may with propriety be regarded as the æra in which that decision is to be made; and a wrong election of the part we shall act, may, in this view, deserve to be considered as the general misfortune of mankind.

This theme was elaborated, the author revealed himself at length as someone who decidedly favored the new Constitution, and he closed by promising a "series of papers" covering six large topics—enough to assure ample and painstaking discussions of union, confederation, energetic government, republican principles, and the preservation of liberty.

These opening promises were reinforced by a number of small but significant touches. "The Federalist" as a running title, for example, was a deft means of casting adversaries under a shadow. The term was not original with Hamilton; he and his correspondents had long used "antifederalist" as a term for those who opposed a strong national government. But in the fall of 1787 the label took on a new connotation. Those who opposed the Constitution might well be good "federalists," loyal supporters of the Articles of Confederation. Many, like "The Federal Farmer," tried to press that advantage. But Hamilton's title linked the word "federalist" with a substantial argument in favor of the Constitution, and so cast its adversaries as "anti-" forces, opponents if not obstructionists. That name has clung to them ever since.[5] The other name attached to the series carried the same positive connotations. Like many other campaign pieces, this first paper was signed with a Roman name, recalling the best of republican virtues from ancient history. But "Publius" was a cut above "Caesar" or "Brutus" or even "Cato." Publius Valerius was not a late defender of the republic but one of its founders. His more famous name, Publicola, meant "friend of the people." Plutarch makes him the Roman parallel to the Greek lawgiver Solon, and claims that he fulfilled Solon's famous dictum on human happiness; his life "so far as human life may be, had been full of all that is good and honourable."[6] Hamilton had used this pseudonym before, in three letters to the press attacking Samuel Chase in 1778. Now he used it to imply a positive, lofty intention behind this new series.

The first essay also stood apart from earlier controversy by appearing in a neutral newspaper. There were five newspapers in New York City at this time. The *Daily Advertiser* and *Morning Post* were dailies; the *Independent Journal* came out on Wednesdays and Saturdays, the *New-York Packet* on

---

[5] For full discussion of this point see Jackson Turner Main, *The Antifederalists: Critics of the Constitution 1781-1788* (1961; rpt. New York, 1974), pp. viii–x; Storing, *Complete Anti-Federalist*, I, 9-11.

[6] *Plutarch's Lives*, Dryden ed., rev. Arthur Hugh Clough, Everyman ed. (London, 1910), I, 160-161.

Tuesdays and Fridays; because of the growing volume of political essays and letters, the *New-York Journal* changed from a weekly to a daily on November 20. None of these papers had a partisan editorial policy. Most were willing to publish any interesting contributions, though the *Morning Post* printed little on the Constitution besides material from newspapers in other states. But Hamilton had recently appeared in the *Daily Advertiser* and the "Caesar" letters had been printed there. "Cato" and "Brutus" were regular features of the Thursday issues of the *New York Journal*. Thus the *Independent Journal* served as a separate, regular, neutral medium for the new *Federalist* series.[7] Papers 1–7 appeared there first as did most of the other installments, though they were regularly reprinted in other newspapers a day or two later. Within the *Independent Journal* these essays stood out, too. The first one filled the last column on page two and part of a column on page three; thereafter the *Federalist* held a regular place in columns one and two on page two—and covered the whole page and more when two installments came out together.

But the most telling feature of the first *Federalist* was a sentence that readers might easily overlook. The next to last paragraph read: "In the progress of this discussion I shall endeavour to give a satisfactory answer to all the objections which shall have made their appearance that may seem to have any claim to your attention." Publius thus committed himself to conduct a long series. He also opened a very nice strategy as a debater. He would not provoke any opposition or try to carry the burden of proof. Instead he would face the worst that opponents could offer against the Constitution and blunt the sharpness of their attacks with calm reason. To carry out this plan, Hamilton ar-

[7] Further details about the contemporary press throughout New York state are surveyed in De Pauw, *Eleventh Pillar*, chap. 6.

ranged to have these essays published and republished as no other series was. It came out twice a week in the *Independent Journal* and then reappeared in the *Daily Advertiser* and the *New-York Packet*. In other words, Hamilton saw to it that these papers not only answered all other commentaries in New York City but answered them in the same pages, reaching the same readers.

This point deserves emphasis because it indicates that the *Federalist* did not emerge to enduring fame by chance or historical coincidence. Hamilton evidently was embarking on a two- or three-part press campaign. First he would answer all immediate opponents by blanketing the New York press. At the same time he would encourage republication in other states. The result would be a comprehensive collection of essays, more far-reaching than any other. It is impossible now to see how he went about arranging the details of this plan, while ensuring that the series remained anonymous. But somehow he did. And so from the first he gave the *Federalist* a conspicuous place in the public debates. It would embrace all other discussions in favor of the Constitution, and all opposing arguments would be ranged against it.

Behind the scenes, Hamilton also enlisted the aid of other writers. Perhaps this was a way of evading sole responsibility if his authorship became known. Perhaps it was a way of ensuring a steady, moderate tone, by tempering his own contributions in collaboration with another. The most likely explanation is that Hamilton simply needed help. He was initiating a complex series at the same time that he was carrying on a law practice and conducting personal political maneuvers toward the ratification convention in his state. Certainly he must have laid his plans for the first issues with John Jay, because Jay immediately wrote Nos. 2–5, which contain echoes and reinforcements of

No. 1. William Duer also wrote a few papers, which have survived though they were not part of the series.[8] Gouverneur Morris recalled being "warmly pressed" by Hamilton to become an author.[9] Perhaps other New Yorkers were approached; Madison has left a hint that Rufus King was mentioned as a possibility.[10] Soon after the series began Jay fell ill and could write no longer. At this point if not earlier, Hamilton approached James Madison. The resulting collaboration made the *Federalist* even larger and more learned.

Madison was in New York as a member of Congress from Virginia. He arrived late in September, was away at Philadelphia briefly in November, and then remained in New York until early March. He and Hamilton were acquainted, on some public issues it is fair to say they had been allied, but they were not close friends. They came from very different backgrounds and their careers were to diverge very widely in just a year or two, but in Philadelphia they had been conspicuous, active delegates. In June Hamilton gave the longest speech of the Convention, a six-hour presentation of his own plan of government, and later he became the sole representative of one of the great states. Madison of course was author of the Virginia Plan, the assiduous recorder of the debates, and a frequent speaker. William Pierce of Georgia recorded his impressions of him as a scholarly, profound politician. "From a spirit of industry and application which he possesses in a most eminent degree, he always comes forward the best informed Man of any point in debate. The affairs of the United States, he perhaps, has the most correct knowledge

[8] They have been printed in *The Federalist*, ed. John C. Hamilton (Philadelphia, 1864), II, 655-659.

[9] Morris to W. H. Wells, February 24, 1815, in Farrand, *Records*, III, 421.

[10] Elizabeth Fleet, ed., "Madison's 'Detatched Memoranda,'" *William and Mary Quarterly*, 3d. ser., 3 (1946), 564-565.

of, of any Man in the Union."[11] In September, William
Samuel Johnson, Hamilton, Madison, Gouverneur Morris, and Rufus King comprised the Committee of Style,
the group that prepared the precise wording of the final
draft. When Hamilton turned to Morris and Madison,
therefore he was calling upon the men who had the most
thorough and intimate command of the new constitution.

Madison's involvement coincided with a further expansion of the *Federalist*. Paper No. 7 concluded with this
announcement: "In order that the whole subject of these
Papers may be as soon as possible laid before the Public, it
is proposed to publish them four times a week, on Tuesday
in the *New-York Packet*, on Wednesday and on Thursday in
the *Daily Advertiser*" (*The Federalist*, ed. Cooke, p. xiii).
Thus the rate of publication was doubled and three newspapers were involved in first publication of single numbers. This schedule could not be maintained exactly, but
three or four papers did appear weekly thereafter. For a
time in December and January the *Federalist* also appeared
in a fourth paper, the *New-York Journal*. Madison contributed, by his reckoning, twenty-six installments plus three
collaborative papers. And the series grew to eighty-five
numbers in the collected edition. Hamilton's son preserved
a letter from the printer which shows that this result far
exceeded original projections. "When I engaged to do the
work," wrote Archibald McLean, "it was to consist of
twenty numbers, or at the utmost twenty-five, which I
agreed to print for thirty pounds—five hundred copies."
This estimate agrees with a remark of Madison's early in
December: "I have not been able to collect all the numbers," he wrote as he sent copies of the *Federalist* columns
to Edmund Randolph, "or I would have sent them to you.

[11]Farrand, *Records*, III, 94.

I have been the less anxious as I understand the Printer means to make a pamphlet of them, when I can give them to you in a more convenient form."[12] That "pamphlet" turned out to be two duodecimo volumes.

Direct evidence about the collaboration between Madison and Hamilton has never come to light. Without it, one can only speculate. But the external outline of the attributions (where both authors agree) encourages a little speculation. Some readers have noticed that Jay's papers (Nos. 2–5 and 64) touch on foreign affairs, an appropriate field for that experienced diplomat. With greater application, Douglass Adair worked out a systematic way of relating Madison's and Hamilton's papers to their speeches and memoranda from the Constitutional Convention. He argues that Hamilton continued to write most of the essays even after Madison joined him, because he was still closely following the outline of the long speech he had made at Philadelphia in June. Madison's first papers (Nos. 10 and 14) are elaborations of ideas he had drafted earlier. Disputed issues (Nos. 18, 19, and 20) cover ideas that both men had prepared in writing before the Convention. (Madison provided a marginal note to No. 18 in the Gideon edition, explaining this procedure.)[13] Thereafter each man worked on the large topics of greatest interest to himself. Hamilton wrote about war powers and taxation (Nos. 23–36); Madison, about liberty and republican forms of government

[12] *The Federalist*, ed. Hamilton, I, lxxxvii; *The Papers of James Madison*, ed. Robert A. Rutland et al., x (Chicago, 1977), 290 (hereafter cited as *PJM*). McLean's letter goes on to say that he priced his subscriptions for the book accordingly at six shillings apiece. This matches the prices in January advertisements in the *Independent Journal*, where McLean still thought the *Federalist* would make one duodecimo volume.

[13] Madison also left a more extensive explanation, quoted by George Bancroft. Both documents are printed and fully discussed in *The Federalist*, ed. Cooke, p. 617.

(Nos. 37–58). Then Madison had to return to Virginia and Hamilton was forced to complete the series alone.[14]

Some of this reasoning is supported by a comparison of the original plan of the *Federalist* with the disposition and headings of the papers in the McLean edition. The six topics Publius promised in paper No. 1 were taken up in the order he listed them, and some of them neatly coincide with the writings of each author:

1. "The utility of the UNION to your political prosperity" (Nos. 2–5 by Jay, on international advantages of union; Nos. 6–9 and 12–13 by Hamilton on domestic advantages; Nos. 10 and 14 by Madison on advantages to libertarian government)
2. "The insufficiency of the present Confederation to preserve that Union" (Nos. 15–22 by Hamilton, with refinements of Nos. 18–20 by Madison)
3. "The necessity of a government at least equally energetic with the one proposed to the attainment of this object" (Nos. 23–36, all by Hamilton)
4. "The conformity of the proposed constitution to the true principles of republican government" (Nos. 37–58 by Madison: Nos. 37–40 on the delicate work of the Convention; 41–44 on the general powers vested in the union; 45–46 on relations between state and federal governments; 47–51 on separation of powers; 52–58 on the House of Representatives. Nos. 59–61 by Hamilton, on elections. Nos. 62–63 disputed; No. 64 by Jay; and Nos. 65–84 by Hamilton: Nos. 62–67 on the Senate; Nos. 68–77 on the president; Nos. 78–83 on the judiciary; and No. 84 on the omission of a bill of rights)

[14] Douglass Adair, *Fame and the Founding Fathers*, ed. Trevor Colbourn (New York, 1974), pp. 49–66.

5. "Its analogy to your own State constitution" (No. 85 by Hamilton)
6. "The additional security which its adoption will afford to the preservation of that species of government, to liberty and to property" (No. 85)

This listing also brings out the fact that the *Federalist* changed its shape in the course of its development. The fourth topic grew from a matter of principle to a practical survey of the central articles of the Constitution. Topics five and six got only an apology at the end. An oddity of phrasing stands out, too. "That species of government" in the sixth topic seems to refer to "the true principles of republican government" in the fourth. In that case, the fifth topic is an interpolation. The discussion of the New York Constitution would, of course, have been a very appropriate topic for Jay or Gouverneur Morris. Perhaps we see in these few lines a bulge of difference that came about from the active participation of Madison and not the others.

But here we have crossed the border into realms of "it may be" and "perhaps." Beyond this point speculation is tantalizing but risky. The *Federalist*, like Shakespeare's sonnets, can be a happy hunting ground for orderly ingenuity. Anyone familiar with periodical publications knows that editorial tinkering produces very misleading appearances. The fact is that the *Federalist*, as a newspaper series, could have been a mosaic of editorial maneuvers. Its crazy publication history strongly indicates that it was: now in one newspaper, now in three; coming out twice a week, then four times, then three (usually); running in four papers, later only in two; broken off in April to be completed in book form in May, then continuing as a serial again in June, July, and August.

Readers who want to trace Madison's or Hamilton's plans

must lean on a collected edition and make simplifying assumptions—that the papers were prepared in haste, in the order they now follow, with scant editorial interference. But there can be no certainty about any of these matters. Madison later wrote that *some* papers were written hurriedly for a press deadline, but he admitted there was close consultation on others; besides, his remarks appear alongside denials that he alone was responsible for what appeared in a collaborative work. Perhaps some papers were prepared well in advance, then touched up to fit into the ongoing sequence. The interval between Nos. 14 and 37 would have given Madison a running start on his long subsequent discussion of federal principles. Jay's No. 64 could have been drafted at the same time as Nos. 2–5. Hamilton's final papers did come out simultaneously before they appeared serially. The order of the papers could have been shuffled accordingly. In fact, some papers were altered between their first appearance and the collected edition. Papers 32 and 33 originally appeared as one long paper. What is now No. 29 was originally No. 35; it makes sense in either position. Since Hamilton and Madison began with notes and memoranda from the Convention, they could have worked very closely without glancing over each other's shoulders. Madison had his own complete transcript of Hamilton's great speech, and he could have lent a copy of some of his own papers. There is an acknowledged overlapping of ideas in Nos. 18–20. In any case, each man was sure to read what had already been published in the series and compose his own paragraphs to suit.

There is even a slight possibility that Madison took a hand in this project very early and helped temper Hamilton's prose as much as Hamilton directed his. Madison wrote to Washington several days before the appearance of No. 10, the first paper he claimed. At that point he en-

closed the first seven numbers and admitted his own involvement. "I will not conceal *from you* that I am likely to
have such *a degree* of connection with the publication here,
as to afford a restraint of delicacy from interesting myself
directly in the republication elsewhere. You will recognize
one of the pens concerned in the task. There are three in
the whole. A fourth may possibly bear a part."[15] This is
deliberately obscure, but some points deserve a second
glance. If Washington is to recognize one of the pens, and
it is not Madison's own, Madison must know that Hamilton already had sent Washington a copy of the first *Federalist* in a letter of October 30. If there are possibly four collaborators, he may be counting Hamilton, Jay, himself,
and Morris (rather than Duer). This letter mentions that
Gouverneur Morris is on his way to Virginia, and will
speak to Washington directly (he arrived at Mount Vernon
the next day). In a letter to Edmund Randolph of the same
date (November 18), Madison states that he returned to
New York "yesterday" from Philadelphia, and that he had
thought of going on to Virginia from there. Adair takes
this to mean that Madison could not have been asked to
join the *Federalist* until after his return (*Fame*, p. 59n83).
But the facts of this letter and its enclosures indicate otherwise—unless Madison heard from Hamilton, made a decision, gathered back numbers, and pored over them just before he sat down to face his correspondence. He must have
been approached before he left New York, that is, some-
time before November 10. If he was involved that early,
why not earlier? Why not at the outset, when the outline of
the series was being developed? There is no way of telling
for certain.

That is the problem. The closer one looks at this collabo-

[15] Madison to Washington, November 18, 1787, *PJM*, x, 254.

ration the more complicated and inscrutable it becomes. Hamilton and Madison are such unlikely partners, so different in their temperaments and later politics, yet these papers are so consistent and so important, that one can strain after any detail trying to unlock their mystery. My own view is that the series represents a complex collaboration, not a sequence of Hamilton's and Madison's quite separate contributions. But of course it is impossible to show this in detail, as well.

What matters, in any case, is that before a dozen papers had seen print the basic outline of the *Federalist* was well established, a complex means of circulation had been engineered, and a working partnership had been struck which would produce a very full account of the Constitution.

Publius and Candor

From these beginnings, a new figure emerged before the eyes of readers in 1787. A public figure who might seem to represent a single, thoughtful author, he was in fact an effective mask for these collaborative efforts, a fictitious, well-calculated spokesman for a new way of understanding constitutional government. To all but a handful of its readers, the *Federalist* was the work of "Publius." And Publius identified himself with a distinctive way of reviewing and weighing all the constitutional arguments a reader was likely to encounter. This general outlook of Publius was, I believe, the most effective means the authors found to hold their series together.

In general Publius laid great stress on two points. One was a reasoned belief in the benefits of government on a large scale—the centralized, extensive government proposed in the Constitution. This idea had both practical and theoretical dimensions; it harmonized an eternal strain between "republican" and "energetic" forms of government; and it grew and developed from paper to paper no matter whose pen was furnishing copy for the press.

Publius's second great theme was a lofty, fair-minded, hopeful attitude toward the new constitution. We have already seen that Hamilton had special reasons for averting provocative or intemperate arguments. But the idea of good-natured, generous, open-minded discussion comes up again and again in these papers. It appears at the beginning and the end, and it stands out in the midst of the most demanding political arguments. Much more than a matter of well-disciplined tone, it seems to be an inherent feature of the authors' common cause, an integral part of their design.

Often this idea is expressed in a word whose meaning has changed since the eighteenth century—the word "candor." This word now denotes forthrightness, frankness, direct honesty. But in the eighteenth century it was more likely to mean almost the opposite: not bold, blunt truth but polite, deferential sweetness of temper. There were in fact two layers of meaning that endured through Voltaire's *Candide* and into the late novels of Jane Austen. One was quiet honesty: "freedom from mental bias, openness of mind; fairness, impartiality, justice" (*OED*). The other was a refined development, a feeling or generous impulse behind disinterestedness: "freedom from malice, favourable disposition, kindliness." Johnson's *Dictionary* defines "candid" in this second sense as "free from malice; not desirous to find faults."

The ratification debates brought this word into frequent use. Perhaps American patriots heard it ringing in the air from the high phrases of the Declaration of Independence: "let facts be submitted to a candid world." Many an essay, at any rate, opened with this idea. The writer of *Letters from the Federal Farmer* promised to study the issues "so far as I am able, with candor and fairness; and leave you to decide upon the propriety of my opinions, the weight of my reasons, and how far my conclusions are well drawn" (Storing, II, 224). The first "Cato" letter urged readers to "deliberate . . . on this new national government with coolness; analize it with criticism; and reflect on it with candour. . . . Beware of those who wish to influence your passions, and to make you dupes to their resentments and little interests—personal invectives can never persuade, but they always fix prejudices which candor might have removed" (Storing, II, 105–106). "Brutus" began with similar sentiments: "I trust the feeble efforts of an individual, to lead the minds of the people to a wise and prudent determination, cannot fail of being acceptable to the candid and dispassionate part of the community" (Storing, II, 363). Anyone analyzing the new constitution would want to seem disinterested; a shrewd debater would also want to persuade readers that they were acting candidly— from pure and generous motives—in siding with him.[16]

The *Federalist*, however, went beyond these tactics to focus on a generous candor that became almost an end in itself. The opening paper makes this attitude the central issue of a proper approach to the Constitution.

---

[16] Tench Coxe wrote Madison in September 1787, explaining that his own essays (by "An American Citizen") were written in a similar vein. "My Object has been to remove apprehensions & to obviate popular reasonings drawn from the public feelings. In doing this in a public Newspaper more attention to those feelings, in the language I have used, was necessary, than if I had addressed a philosophic mind" (*PJM*, x, 175). It is worth noting that this letter addresses both Madison and Hamilton, and encourages them to reprint Coxe's essays in newspapers of New York and Virginia.

In a long central paragraph, the word appears for the first time—to warn readers away from the wild zeal of adversaries, but also to admit, very generously, that truth and motives for zeal can make strange combinations.

> I am well aware that it would be disingenuous to resolve indiscriminately the opposition of any set of men (merely because their situations might subject them to suspicion) into interested or ambitious views: Candour will oblige us to admit, that even such men may be actuated by upright intentions; and it cannot be doubted that much of the opposition which has made its appearance, or may hereafter make its appearance, will spring from sources, blameless at least, if not respectable, the honest errors of minds led astray by preconceived jealousies and fears. So numerous indeed and so powerful are the causes, which serve to give a false bias to the judgment, that we, upon many occasions, see wise and good men on the wrong as well as on the right side of questions, of the first magnitude to society. This circumstance, if duly attended to, would furnish a lesson in moderation to those, who are ever so much persuaded of their being in the right, in any controversy. And a further reason for caution, in this respect, might be drawn from the reflection, that we are not always sure, that those who advocate the truth are influenced by purer principles than their antagonists.

Of course Publius moves on promptly to suppose that truth and safety are most likely to be found among partisans of strong government; to acknowledge frankly that these papers "proceed from a source not unfriendly to the new Constitution." But this fair-minded wavering at the outset is ample and generous, and it leads to a promise which Publius was scrupulous to observe: "My arguments will be open to all, and may be judged of by all. They shall at least be offered in a spirit, which will not disgrace the cause of truth."

In the long run, Publius directs the reader's candor not only toward himself and his arguments, but also toward the Constitution and the sources from which it sprang. He is prompt to develop the notion that the Convention itself had been specially blessed by concord, respect, civility, and sober deliberation. "This Convention, composed of men, who possessed the confidence of the people, and many of whom had become highly distinguished by their patriotism, virtue and wisdom, in times which tried the minds and hearts of men, undertook the arduous task. In the mild season of peace, with minds unoccupied by other subjects, they passed many months in cool uninterrupted and daily consultations: and finally, without having been awed by power, or influenced by any passions except love for their Country, they presented and recommended to the people the plan produced by their joint and very unanimous counsels." These words from paper No. 2 form part of a steady chain of reasoning in favor of "that sedate and candid consideration, which the magnitude and importance of the subject demand, and which it certainly ought to receive." Later Publius dwells on how important it is to catch the fleeting occasion for a stable constitution. In No. 49 he insists that constitutional questions are too ticklish to be brought often before the public.

We are to recollect that all the existing [state] constitutions were formed in the midst of a danger which repressed the passions most unfriendly to order and concord; of an enthusiastic confidence of the people in their patriotic leaders, which stifled the ordinary diversity of opinions on great national questions; of a universal ardor for new and opposite forms, produced by a universal resentment and indignation against the antient government; and whilst no spirit of party, connected with the changes to be made, or the abuses to be reformed, could mingle its leven in the operation. The future situations in which we must expect to be usually placed, do not present any equivalent security.

Again, in discussing the compromise of popular representation in the House and state representation in the Senate, he ascribes it to "a spirit of amity, and that mutual deference and concession which the peculiarity of our political situation rendered indispensable" (No. 62).[17]

On theoretical grounds, the *Federalist* argues that this spirit of mutual deference runs against ordinary human nature. The celebrated paper on faction, No. 10, argues that "the latent causes of faction are . . . sown in the nature of man." The reason of man is fallible and subject to the pressures of passion and self-love. Men join together most naturally for advantages which are "adverse to the rights of other citizens, or to the permanent and aggregate interests of the community." For this reason, society is constantly divided into fragments or short-sighted interest groups, and the chief task of modern legislation is to regulate these interfering interests and direct their energies to the common good. Enlightened statesmen, even if such rare talents happen to be in power, cannot overcome this situation by themselves. They must be aided and sustained by the structure of a constitutional republic. Only by entrusting

[17] These words appear in quotation marks in the *Federalist* and refer to George Washington's covering letter, with which he submitted the Constitution to Congress (Farrand, *Records*, II, 667). Similar sentiments were expressed by many members of the Convention; see the citations listed in ibid., p. 16n4.

power to delegates, and by drawing governmental officers from a large geographical territory, can a people hope to control the effects of faction. Under these limitations, no faction can grow large or strong enough to impose its will on the nation; thus "we behold a Republican remedy for the diseases most incident to Republican Government." Pressed to its logical conclusion, however, this line of argument leads to an enormous new problem. For if disinterestedness is so rare among men in society—if indeed its opposite, factional interest, provides the energy necessary to animate popular government—how can a wisely designed constitution arise and come to control the endless, chaotic struggles for power among local demagogues and partisan alliances?

This problem remained unresolved as Publius continued to reason his way through these papers. Looking to antiquity in No. 38, he saw that in every government that ruled by consent of the governed, the task of framing a constitution fell to a single wise, just statesman. The task was too delicate, the difficulties too large, to risk dissension among collaborators. And in the end even Solon and Lycurgus resorted to compromise and stratagem to complete their work. There was no other way to bring disinterested wisdom within the grasp of ordinary men. Viewed in this light, the Philadelphia Convention was a prodigy in history. Only a candid eye could see properly into its disinterested work and, further, into the hopeful balance of compromises it had reached. The ideal readers of the *Federalist* "will proceed to an examination of the plan submitted by the Convention, not only without a disposition to find or to magnify faults; but will see the propriety of reflecting that a faultless plan was not to be expected. Nor will they barely make allowances for the errors which may be chargeable on the fallibility to which the Convention, as

[67]

a body of men, were liable; but will keep in mind that they themselves also are but men, and ought not to assume an infallibility in rejudging the fallible opinions of others" (No. 37). This same paper plainly expresses the problem the Convention faced in overcoming the impediments of faction. A variety of factional interests, "for reasons sufficiently explained in a former paper, may have a salutary influence on the administration of the Government when formed; yet everyone must be sensible of the contrary influence which must have been experienced in the task of forming it."

> The real wonder is, that so many difficulties should have been surmounted; and surmounted with a unanimity almost as unprecedented as it must have been unexpected. It is impossible for any man of candor to reflect on this circumstance, without partaking of the astonishment. It is impossible for the man of pious reflection not to perceive in it, a finger of that Almighty hand which has been so frequently and signally extended to our relief in the critical stages of the revolution.

If candor thus led to astonishment and even awe at the work of the Convention, the same spirit might accomplish yet more in the moment at hand. A paper constitution had been completed at Philadelphia, but it was still to be established as the basis of American life. Ratification remained uncertain as the *Federalist* was being written, and beyond lay the difficulties of turning words into deeds, clauses into precedents, the consent of a majority into sustained acceptance by a nation. "'Tis time only that can mature and perfect so compound a system, can liquidate the meaning of all the parts, and can adjust them to each other in a harmonious and consistent WHOLE" (No. 82). In such a delicate political situation, it was essential to develop a national spirit of good will. The Constitution obviously had to survive the worst attacks generated in the struggle over ratification, but to carry authority it also had to rise above them. The *Federalist*, in turn, had to be more than trenchant, and its authors had to see beyond the winning of a few grudged ballots or narrow majorities. They had to dispel doubt, elicit assent, and promote a lasting sense of confidence in the new framework of government.

Thus candor developed as a mood directed outward from Publius toward his opponents. But Publius stood as an ethical model, too, for the conduct and attitudes readers should adopt in return. He worked to elicit feelings of candor not only toward himself, or the *Federalist* papers, but also toward the work of the Convention, the new constitution, and the national government that would grow from its ratification.

The discipline of candor in the *Federalist* took form in three practical strategies. The first was a stress on positive achievements, the second an appearance of rigid rationalism, and the third a display of restraint and patience in the face of unwarranted attacks. With some overlapping, these strategies coincide with discussions of the advantages of union (Nos. 2–14), needs beyond Confederation (Nos. 15–36), and the structure of the Constitution (Nos. 37–85).

Confirmation of Patriotic Union

The strong emphasis on candor which opens the *Federalist* was followed by a very positive discussion of the idea of union. In their hearts, the writers may have felt that the Constitution provided a patched-up alternative to chaos.

Their private papers show them worrying about what would happen if ratification failed. They imagined the worst, a breaking up of the states, and they dwelled on sectional rivalries and local jealousies that were already making government unworkable. But here they take a very different tone. They do not begin by pointing out defects. They point out strengths, and paint them in warm shades of patriotism and progress. Instead of finding fault with the Articles of Confederation, they begin by noticing the common geography, language, history, and origins that bind the peoples of all the states. They trace the success of their common efforts in war and peace.

Publius leaves it to others to criticize or suggest that the Constitution is an attempt to usurp the powers of the states. He assumes that union is already producing advantages and that the opponents of the Constitution would destroy that harmony. "It has until lately been a received and uncontradicted opinion, that the prosperity of the people of America depended on their continuing firmly united, and the wishes, prayers, and efforts of our best and wisest Citizens have been constantly directed to that object. But Politicians now appear, who insist that this opinion is erroneous, and that instead of looking for safety and happiness in union, we ought to seek it in a division of the States into distinct confederacies or sovereignties" (No. 2). The argument is of course specious; no politicians were overtly campaigning against union. But by opening in this way Publius created a very appealing outline, reviewing advantages of union against the threats of foreign intervention and internal disorder, appealing to feelings already "deeply engraved on the hearts of the great body of the people in every state" (No. 1), and recalling the principles and sacrifices of the Revolution. He also handily inverted the easiest line of criticism, that the Constitution was a dangerous innovation:

> Hearken not to the voice which petulantly tells you that the form of government recommended for your adoption is a novelty in the political world. . . . Shut your hearts against the poison which it conveys; the kindred blood which flows in the veins of American citizens, the mingled blood which they have shed in defence of their sacred rights, consecrate their union, and excite horror at the idea of their becoming aliens, rivals, enemies. And if novelties are to be shunned, believe me the most alarming of all novelties, the most wild of all projects, the most rash of all attempts, is that of rending us in pieces, in order to preserve our liberties and promote our happiness.   [No. 14]

For its first month the *Federalist* thus came before the public to reaffirm old truths while looking hopefully to both the past and future.

Arguments from High Principle

Eventually Publius had to engage in attack and criticism, to describe the insufficiency of Confederation. But at this point he turned to another strategy in order to maintain an affirmative tone. He does not belabor particular failures in the old Congress or state governments, sectional grievances, and other worries. He argues from principle. And he states and illustrates principles that range far beyond the current situation.

The weakness of Confederation is itself presented as a proposition on which all candid reasoners must agree. "It may perhaps be asked, what need is there of reasoning or proof to illustrate a position, which is not either controverted or doubted; to which the understandings and feelings of all classes of men assent; and which in substance is admitted by the opponents as well as by the friends of the New Constitution?" (No. 15). Publius then contends that two radical principles must be observed in a strong government: a national government should have power directly over citizens rather than merely over its member states; and some of these national powers should be unlimited. "The great and radical vice in the construction of the existing Confederation," reads No. 15, "is in the principle of LEGISLATION for STATES or GOVERNMENTS, in their CORPORATE or COLLECTIVE CAPACITIES and as contradistinguished from the INDIVIDUALS of whom they consist." This point is developed in a series of papers with examples drawn from confederacies ancient and modern. Then, by turning directly to the need for powers of common defense, a case is made for energetic government. "These powers ought to exist without limitation," No. 23 states emphatically: "*Because it is impossible to foresee or define the extent and variety of national exigencies, or the corresponding extent & variety of the means which may be necessary to satisfy them.*" This idea is not illustrated with historical examples because Publius insists that it rests on sheer self-evidence. "This is one of those truths, which to a correct and unprejudiced mind, carries its own evidence along with it; and may be obscured, but cannot be made plainer by argument or reasoning. It rests upon axioms as simple as they are universal. The *means* ought to be proportioned to the *end*; the persons, from whose agency the attainment of any *end* is expected, ought to possess the *means* by which it is to be attained."

This appeal to self-evidence and "axioms" also appears at this point in many individual papers. No. 31 devotes considerable space to the idea of such reasoning. "In disquisitions of every kind," it begins, "there are certain primary truths or first principles upon which all subsequent reasonings must depend. These contain an internal evidence, which antecedent to all reflection or combination commands the assent of the mind." Such truths are well known in geometry, and there are maxims "of the same nature" in ethics and politics. Furthermore, "there are other truths in the two latter sciences, which if they cannot pretend to rank in the class of axioms, are yet such direct inferences from them, and so obvious in themselves, and so agreeable to the natural and unsophisticated dictates of common sense, that they challenge the assent of a sound and unbiassed mind, with a degree of force and conviction almost equally irresistable."

Of course such a display of almost geometrical reasoning has a very practical purpose here. It not only maintains a positive tone but also gives strength to a very delicate part of the argument. Publius is arguing for unlimited federal powers over armies and taxes, and he must call on every resource to make his case seem reasonable and necessary. But as Morton White has shown, he is not therefore being extraordinarily sophistical. Rigorous reasoning from "maxims" or self-evidence was often practiced in the political essays of early America. It stands out at the opening of the Declaration of Independence: "We hold these truths to be self-evident." It figures in many revolutionary pamphlets, including two by Hamilton. It can be traced to philosophical writings which were commonly read in the colonies—works by Locke, Burlemaqui, Hume, and others. Publius is therefore speaking a familiar language, even though he is not practicing an unassailable logic.[18]

Answers to Objections

The third strategy of candor picks up Publius's early promise to his readers and applies it to a full discussion of the Constitution. He had said he would "give a satisfactory answer to all the objections" that were worth noticing. From paper No. 39 onward he could turn this promise to advantage. When Hamilton and Madison had begun the series, they both had the benefit of notes and memoranda from the Convention. But much of this material was now exhausted and the demands of the printers continued to press upon them. Under these circumstances, the clamor of the opposition provided Publius with some welcome assistance. By taking up the chief arguments that had already been made on a subject, he could readily provide himself with a clear focus. Furthermore, he could shift the burden of his argument very conveniently, without sacrificing its continuous development. Earlier he had had to attack Confederation while seeming to affirm its basic principles of union and representative government. Now he had to explain the Constitution without reducing it too compactly; it would not do to suggest it was a product of a new and rigorous theory. In dealing with Confederation, Publius had been able to assert his own authority in interpreting a common experience. But discussing the Constitution

[18] Morton White, *The Philosophy of the American Revolution* (New York, 1978), pp. 78–94.

presented a different challenge. This document was not yet common to public knowledge or experience; it was still being developed. It already went beyond the plans that Hamilton, Madison, or anyone else had brought to the Convention and it still had to survive the test of nine or more ratifications. Even then it might be amended (with perhaps a bill of rights), and it would surely be modified by the actual establishment of a federal government. For now, its clauses called for interpretation that would be clear but not rigid, precise but not narrow. Hamilton and Madison were exceptionally well prepared for detailed argument of just this sort. And if there was a danger of becoming too detailed, it was offset by the fact that there were to be more than thirty of these papers, progressing steadily through the sections of the Constitution on "the several parts of the government" (No. 52).

The edge of argument in these later papers thus arose from the antifederalists, to be smoothed by an expert Publius. Candor was observed by blunting and absorbing attacks so that argument might end in justified agreement.

Publius began the reconciliation by looking beyond persons to issues, and drawing the latter into the full light of day. He practiced severe restraint toward particular adversaries, almost never mentioning names or otherwise calling attention to the exact source of any attack on the Constitution. Frequently he made arguments seem widely held by imputing them broadly to "the adversaries of the plan of the Convention." He might take note that various (unspecified) groups objected to the same point for different reasons. He might distinguish "the more respectable adversaries" (No. 47), "the most intelligent of those who have found fault" (No. 76), or even "the more candid opposers" (No. 61). But proper names are rare. I have found

[75]

them in only five papers, and they are raised there mainly to clarify some marginal observations.[19]

To completely absorb attacks, Publius was also careful to state them fully and allow for the most contingent circumstances in which they might prove telling. An especially good example of this thoroughness can be found in No. 44. This paper takes up the "necessary and proper" clause (Article I, section 8, clause 18), which seems to grant blanket powers beyond those enumerated in the same section of the Constitution. Publius denies that excessive powers are granted here, and the method of his answer is characteristic.[20] First he tries to imagine the possible alternative means that might have been used to the same end. "There are four other possible methods which the Convention might have taken on this subject." One by one he names them, and one by one he shows that each of them leads to unacceptable consequences. Then he goes further. What if Congress misconstrues this part of the Constitution? He describes a remedy in the separation of federal powers and in the balance between the states and the federal government. Then he goes further still, by noticing another similar provision—the "supreme law of the land" clause (Article VI, clause 2)—and giving three prompt arguments in its defense. In short, Publius not only returns a sufficient answer, but also penetrates beyond the immediate objection into the depth of the worry that prompts it.

Even when an adversary's charges seem strained and far-fetched Publius leans out to catch and respond to them. "The only refuge left for those who prophesy the downfall

---

[19] Nos. 67, 69, 73, 78, 83. No. 67 does lambaste "Cato" directly, as we shall see.

[20] There is another treatment of this clause in the discussion of taxation (No. 33); it too develops by answering question after question about this provision, and allows the worst by relating it to the "supreme law" clause.

of the State Governments," reads No. 46, "is the visionary supposition that the Fœderal Government may previously accumulate a military force for the projects of ambition." Is this remark an out-of-hand dismissal of such prophets? No, their position is attacked here as absurd on its face, but the paragraph goes on to meet it even so. "Extravagant as the supposition is, let it however be made." The *Federalist* has a further answer ready in that case, too. Similar concessions can be found at the close of Nos. 40, 60, 63, and 64.

Sometimes the effort of sustaining this candor even forces the authors into antic poses. *Federalist* No. 54 discusses the tricky provision in Article 1 for counting three-fifths of the slave population in calculating taxation and representation. This was a naked compromise between North and South, without any good principle to support it. But Publius weighs it very seriously. He begins by condensing the leading objection: "Slaves are considered as property, not as persons. They ought therefore to be comprehended in estimates of taxation which are founded on property, and to be excluded from representation which is regulated by a census of persons. This is the objection, as I understand it, stated in its full force." But to answer the objection, Publius invokes yet a further mask. "I shall be equally candid," he says, "in stating the reasoning which may be offered on the opposite side" from "one of our southern brethren." This manifestly fictitious slaveholder is quoted through several paragraphs, and in the end Publius concludes that though such reasoning "may appear to be a little strained in some points, yet on the whole, I must confess, that it fully reconciles me to the scale of representation, which the Convention have established." If Madison wrote this paper, as he claimed, he is here straining as a constitutionalist while regarding himself, as a slaveholder, at arm's length.

Another great strain shows in No. 67, the first in a series

on the presidency. Here, for once, Publius lashes out at a particular foe, the fifth letter of "Cato." Cato had charged that the president would be like a monarch. Publius replies by hammering at a very small mistake of information in Cato's discussion, citing it as a typical misrepresentation. No part of the Constitution, he says, has been attacked with so little candor; it is therefore necessary not only to face perversity here, but to unmask it.

> In the execution of this task there is no man, who would not find it an arduous effort, either to behold with moderation or to treat with seriousness the devices, not less weak than wicked, which have been contrived to pervert the public opinion in relation to the subject. They so far exceed the usual, though unjustifiable, licenses of party-artifice, that even in a disposition the most candid and tolerant they must force the sentiments which favor an indulgent construction of political adversaries to give place to a voluntary and unreserved indignation.

At the end of the paper he apologizes again: "Nor have I scrupled in so flagrant a case to allow myself a severity of animadversion little congenial with the general spirit of these papers." Thus does Publius both press against the limits of his own decorum and yet hold himself in check after all.

It has often been remarked that the *Federalist* papers take a consistent view of human nature as depraved, treacherous, in need of strong government. But the persistent discipline of candor in this series tells another story. It reaffirms, in doctrine and practice, something that Publius states clearly in No. 55: "As there is a degree of depravity in mankind which requires a certain degree of circumspection and distrust: So there are other qualities in human nature, which justify a certain portion of esteem and confidence. Republican government presupposes the existence of these qualities in a higher degree than any other form." As he looked back upon the completed series in No. 85, Publius could congratulate himself, too.

> Thus have I, my fellow citizens, executed the task I had assigned to myself; with what success, your conduct must determine. I trust at least you will admit, that I have not failed in the assurance I gave you respecting the spirit in which my endeavours should be conducted. I have addressed myself purely to your judgments, and have studiously avoided those asperities which are too apt to disgrace political disputants of all parties, and which have been not a little provoked by the language and conduct of opponents of the constitution. . . . It is certain that I have frequently felt a struggle between sensibility and moderation, and if the former has in some instances prevailed, it must be my excuse that it has been neither often nor much.

CHAPTER THREE

The Authority of Publius

After surveying the reputation and form of the *Federalist* we come to the question of its authority, in its own time and in ours. What is the basis, if any, of a legitimate respect for these papers? In what sense do they deserve careful reading and repay formal study? So far we have looked very critically at claims that they contain definitive arguments about American politics. Why then should they hold our attention? And most acutely, what kind of authority do they have? By authority I mean the power to influence other minds, to draw on such wide experience and deep knowledge that others come to rely on one's judgment. A parent exercises authority rather than mere control when he or she understands children well and can point out the best alternatives for their growth. A teacher gains authority when he not only demonstrates mastery of a subject but also has a sense of how it will change in time and how students can learn along with him. Political authority rests on a leader's capacity to coordinate a people's will and direct it to their lasting well-being. Is there such a power in these papers, is it more than specious, and how does it relate to the Constitution?

Political Authority

Earlier we looked at four ways in which the *Federalist* could not be fully credited with authority—as a decisive force in the ratification campaign, as an expression of Hamilton's or Madison's beliefs, as a record of the Founders' intentions, or as a work of rigorous philosophy. But the last word has not yet been said on any of these matters. As they are usually explained, these approaches to the *Federalist* are misleading because they regard this work mainly as a closed book, as a collection of definitive statements. As an essay series, however, the *Federalist* appears in another light. It does not stand frozen in history, between the Convention in Philadelphia and Washington's inauguration in Wall Street; it comes to life as an effort on the part of the authors as well as their readers, to make sense of a new form of government and test the phrases of an untried document in public debate.

The *Federalist* is not effective as propaganda, if its force is measured by the number of votes it could gain for ratification. But as a campaign effort, as an attempt to meet and answer all other campaign literature, it is hard to see how it could have been surpassed. Hamilton tried to enlist the best-informed writers available to him. He outlined a comprehensive treatment of the Constitution and the conditions that had brought it forth. Together with Jay and Madison, he labored at a series longer than any other. And these writers deliberately took notice of the criticisms that were circulating and tried to address them. Some of their answers are strained, narrow, rhetorical, or legalistic. But at least they are what they claim to be—thoughtful, well-informed, public answers to the large range of doubts that the new Constitution was raising. Moreover, the consistent high tone of the series served as a damper on the violence of the ratification debate; it still shows three important writers laboring to assert calm reason through several months, whether they were read or not.

In this respect, the odd publishing arrangements for the *Federalist* also deserve a second glance. It may seem that publication in four out of five city newspapers, and republication (for a time) in distant Boston, Philadelphia, and Richmond add up to a pushy strategy for outshining all other pamphlets or essay series. Subscribers to one New York newspaper raised the issue explicitly. They charged that such blanket coverage was but "a new mode of abridging the liberty of the press," and asked the editor not to "encourage the presumptive attempt of that author to occupy the greater portion of the public high-way than decently comes to his share" (*New-York Journal*, January 1, 1788). The *Federalist* might have been such a pushy work, if it had been arranged by different writers for a different end. But these authors certainly knew that they were presenting special expertise, and when they wrote to others they explained that their work would be long and temperate. "The constitution proposed has in this state warm friends and warm enemies," Hamilton wrote to Washington. "The first impressions everywhere are in its favour; but the artillery of its opponents makes some impression. The event cannot yet be foreseen. The inclosed is the first number of a series of papers to be written in its defence." The accent, as in the first paper itself, is on defense. Less than three weeks later, Madison stressed fullness: "If the whole plan should be executed, it will present to the public a full discussion of the merits of the proposed Constitution in all its relations." Still later Madison apologized for being unable to "collect all the numbers" to send Edmund Randolph, because this series "proposes to go through the sub-

ject."[1] In its own terms, the *Federalist* was not an assault
but a comprehensive defense, and its widespread diffusion
can be seen as a fair tactic of defensive thoroughness. It
was a way of meeting critics directly, in the same papers,
before the same readers—just as letters to the editor still
answer one another today.

We must remember that this particular campaign situation worked against a very clear or productive national debate. Once Congress submitted the Constitution to the
states, ratification was a slow and fragmentary process of
state conventions, local politics, and disparate exchanges in
the press. Apart from networks of private correspondence
there was no coordinated campaign, no truly national presentation on either side. Because of slow transportation and
communications between the states, and because the issue
itself involved interstate rivalries and suspicions, nothing
of the sort can be imagined. The closest approximations
seem to have been an enormous distribution of the anti-
federalist pamphlet, *Letters from the Federal Farmer*, and the
steady development and eventual publication of the completed *Federalist* series. Whether designedly or not, the *Federalist* therefore helped to raise the constitutional debates to
something like common national attention. By answering
so comprehensively, it gave place and arrangement to ideas
that might otherwise have flickered only briefly here and
there. By appearing in several papers, in several states, and
later in a solid collection, it encouraged discussion of those
same ideas far along the seaboard and beyond the time

[1] Hamilton to Washington, October 30, 1787, in *The Papers of Alexander Hamilton*, ed. Harold C. Syrett and Jacob E. Cooke, 24 vols. (New
York, 1961–1979), IV, 306; Madison to Washington, November 18,
1787, and Madison to Randolph, December 2, 1787, in *The Papers of
James Madison*, ed. Robert A. Rutland et al., x (Chicago, 1977), 254,
290.

of formal ratification. Publius not only participated in a great debate; his emergence was one of the aspects of its greatness.

The transcending of state boundaries, of course, coincides nicely with the collaboration that developed between an aggressive New Yorker and a scholarly Virginian. Neither Hamilton nor Madison could endorse the entire *Federalist*; neither could stand by all that he alone wrote for it. But together they made more than a collaboration; they made an alliance. To judge from his earliest forays, Hamilton alone might have produced the *Federalist* as a sheaf of fifteen or twenty essays, gradually growing more polemical as he addressed fellow New Yorkers. Madison, on the other hand, might have published nothing at all, but filed his reams of convention notes and private memoranda away in his study while preparing for debates in Richmond. Harnessed together behind Publius, both men assumed different characters while exercising their several talents. They balanced not only regional interests but divergent temperaments. Hamilton the shrewd publicist and lawyer joined forces with the most assiduous student of congresses and confederacies. The *Federalist* therefore carries an edge of refined discussion, of arguments sharpened and purified by the tension of these contrary impulses. At its core is a bond of strong agreement—on the defensible merits of the Constitution.

And this cause actually developed in these authors' hands. Madison later saw very clearly that no one could ever discern what the framers of the Constitution had intended. The framers could not know it themselves. The Convention, like any large meeting, was a gathering of various understandings and motivations. The states were represented in it very unevenly. Rhode Island had refused to send anyone. There were odd splits and combinations within delegations when they came to vote on various issues. A few men came forward very energetically. Others said little. At the end some refused to sign, some were persuaded in the course of debate, some went away and had second thoughts. No one could be completely satisfied with the final draft. Probably only a handful of men understood it in full detail.

In defending this new Constitution, Hamilton and Madison thus had to construe it as no one else had done or could do. They had been alert observers at the Convention, as well as participants. Madison was to boast of his records that they caught not only substance but nuance. "In the labor and correctness of this I was not a little aided by practice [he had kept similar notes of Congressional debates], and by a familiarity with the style and train of observation and reasoning which characterized the principal speakers. It happened, also, that I was not absent a single day, nor more than a casual fraction of an hour in any day, so that I could not have lost a single speech, unless a very short one."[2] Now the *Federalist* provided a framework for such keen political observation; it drew Hamilton and Madison out before a public to whom the Constitution was entirely new. They would not break their pledge (or betray their anonymity) by reporting the debates they had witnessed. But they were in a special position to bring informed intelligence to the explication of this document.

In a sense, they began to explain it to themselves. Neither author was completely satisfied, or even tolerably hopeful, when he left the Convention. As a result, the act of writing a defense of the Constitution was an exercise in self-contradiction—or perhaps better said, self-persuasion.

[2] Max Farrand, ed., *The Records of the Federal Convention of 1787*, rev. ed. (New Haven, 1937), III, 550.

The task imposed on Publius required Hamilton and Madison to review the Constitution, to go over it once more in a spirit of candor, looking for strengths rather than defects. As collaborators, they had to sustain, answer, and reinforce each other; they had to imagine and agree upon how the words and clauses of a compromise document could come to life in a strong and active government. They had to state their reasoning plainly and fully, under the eyes of readers who might be sharply critical if not personally hostile.

This exercise, of course, was a way of strengthening each man's hands for the years that followed. When the new government did take form under Washington, Hamilton and Madison were remarkably well prepared to become conspicuous national statesmen. Already they had rehearsed the Constitution to themselves, committed themselves to it in print, line by line. Moreover, they had gone through months of thinking and writing about it in a new language, the national, constitutional accents of Publius rather than the dialects of local politics and state ratifications alone.[3]

Again, the difference is narrow but important. The *Fed-*

---

[3] It is worth pondering that other effective leaders of early administrations had also been forced to think and speak responsibly beyond their home regions: Washington as military commander of the Revolution; Franklin, Adams, Jefferson, Jay, Charles Pinckney, and Rufus King as ministers abroad. Hamilton and Madison stand out as figures who did *not* have either a military command, a governorship, or a foreign mission before taking on major roles under the Constitution. Both, of course, had been members of Congress. In fact both men were in their early thirties in 1787, and were overshadowed by other great men. Hamilton was sometimes written off as a former aide to Washington and the son-in-law of General Philip Schuyler. Madison was certainly not the most illustrious Virginian in the era of Washington, Mason, Rutledge, Jefferson, Henry, George Wythe, and R. H. Lee. In his own home he was emphatically James Madison, Junior; that is the style with which he signed his letters.

eralist does not represent the fixed intentions of the framers of the Constitution. But it does embody the *developing* intentions of two of them—two of the most active, articulate, reflective, and well-informed men who ever joined forces or crossed each other in American politics.

Finally, the form and authorship of the *Federalist* make it an astonishing record of early American political thinking. Although it is not a consistent presentation of mature theory, it is still an extraordinary effort of mature political practice. The ratification process was in itself a great appeal to the sovereignty of the people through specially elected representatives. The *Federalist* goes one step further, and appeals for informed assent. It makes a public display of ample discussion of the issues. It reveals not only the voters but the framers in the act of deliberating. This, I believe, is the most enduring source of its authority. Its pages still hold the tension of arguments that are not conclusive. The authors and readers are both hesitating for a long interval between an unsatisfactory past and an uncertain future. What they share—what they must make an effort to share—is recognition of common doubts, a healthy circumspection, and yet a strong impulse to press forward in affirmation of a new and stronger identity.

Literate Mental Warfare

The *Federalist* is not the only work that exercises this kind of authority. To understand it completely we must also look at similar works beyond the campaigns of 1787–1788, though not beyond the confines of publications in English in this general period. A hundred years earlier, a serial publication of this kind could not have been undertaken. A few decades later, it would have lost its force in a welter of commonplace newspapers and newspaper columns and editorials. But the eighteenth century witnessed the rise, development, and impact of many papers like the *Federalist*—pseudonymous, regular, widely distributed essays, addressing social issues for a new public of citizen-readers.

Modern readers are so accustomed to daily newspapers that they may begin with a wrong idea of such publications. Or they may read edited selections of essays in this form and suppose that they were penned at leisure by gentlemen in brocade and powdered wigs. The fact is that these publications usually came out as publishing ventures— projects that tested the finances and political daring of their authors and printers. The basic right to print social or political criticism was still a novelty. The idea of addressing an informed reading public was still being explored and refined by a new generation of writers and politicians.

Freedom of the press was most extensive in England in the eighteenth century, but even so it had limits. Until 1695 the Licensing Act had controlled all publishing; thereafter the government found other effective methods short of censorship. Attacks on the government or its chief officers could be prosecuted for seditious libel, and until the end of the century it was up to the judge, not the jury, to decide whether the work was in fact libelous. Parliamentary debates could not be reported, under penalties for breach of privilege; these same sanctions were sometimes used against other publications. And as early as 1712 a stamp tax was passed to cripple newspapers by taxing every sheet of paper on which they were printed and every advertisement that they carried.[4]

---

[4] These matters are surveyed in Frederick Seaton Siebert, *Freedom of the Press in England 1476–1776* (Urbana, Ill., 1952; rpt. 1965), and E. Neville Williams, *The Eighteenth-Century Constitution 1688–1815: Documents and Commentary* (Cambridge, 1960), pp. 397–407, 133–148.

Nevertheless, newspapers, broadsides, and political essay papers began to flourish in the reign of Queen Anne, and ingenious writers and printers found dozens of ways of pushing against government controls. They might print only a single sheet of paper on a handpress, distribute only a few hundred copies, and make a very small profit. But there was always the chance that they would touch what we now call public opinion. For decades that temptation proved irresistible. Almost every major author of the century put his skills into short, cheap, serial papers criticizing public life. Defoe, Swift, Addison, Steele, Pope, Fielding, Johnson, Goldsmith, Boswell—all of them wrote periodical essays behind the protection of anonymity or a pseudonym. Almost all of them experimented with this form, too, trying to find a more telling way of inculcating morality or a political persuasion.

Many of these essays were reprinted or circulated in the colonies and collections of them were read. Benjamin Franklin remembered learning to perfect his style as a boy, by modeling his earliest essays on the *Spectator* papers. Forty years later Madison did almost the same. He made a point of it in his brief sketch of autobiography: "One of the earliest books which engaged his attention was the 'Spectator,' which from his own experience, he inferred to be peculiarly adapted to inculcate in youthful minds, just sentiments[,] an appetite for knowledge, and a taste for the improvement of the mind and manners."[5] More to the point, the efforts of writers and polemicists to gain freedom of the press in England came to reinforce other struggles for liberty in America. Readers who did not have leisure to pore over the *Spectator* or the *Rambler* were still

[5] *The Autobiography of Benjamin Franklin*, ed. Leonard W. Labaree et al. (New Haven, 1964), pp. 61–62; "James Madison's Autobiography," ed. Douglass Adair, *William and Mary Quarterly*, 3d ser., 2 (1945), 197.

likely to know other series that had erupted in London and later crossed the ocean in bound volumes. Swift's *Examiner* was still being imitated during the ratification debates; so was Addison's *Old Whig*. The "Cato" letters of John Trenchard and Thomas Gordon had been a sourcebook of political liberalism since the 1720s. The *North Briton* of John Wilkes was famous throughout the colonies in the 1760s, as the letters of "Junius" were in the 1770s.

With the coming of revolution American patriots wrote political series of their own. To name only a few of the more famous: John Adams, twelve "Novanglus" papers in the *Massachusetts Gazette* (1775); John Dickinson, twelve "Letters from a Farmer in Pennsylvania" in the *Pennsylvania Chronicle and Universal Advertiser* (1767); Thomas Paine, numerous papers including four letters of "Forester" in defense of *Common Sense* and the opening installment of the *Crisis* pamphlets (*Pennsylvania Journal*, 1776). These and many other papers and pamphlets gave readers in America ample schooling in political matters. They quoted legal precedents and philosophical authorities; they cited ancient and modern examples; they appealed to common sentiments and imagined future prospects; and they dared to be extensive and scholarly, examining the nature of the British constitution and proposing action to make a more just society in the New World. Following these many predecessors, the *Federalist* and other ratification papers were not so much breaking new ground as carrying a familiar form of discourse to its highest development.

The periodical press was evidently supplanting other forms of authority. Its full potency could be felt, though it was not always articulated. Year by year, legal test by legal test, pages of ordinary newsprint were gaining more subscribers, reaching out to touch more minds. They were thus slowly undermining more traditional forms of national communication and influence—pulpit, parliament, and crown. Franklin and Madison are quite forthright in saying that they changed their minds and manners over the pages of the *Spectator*. They stayed away from church and gave themselves to books. Later in the century it was also manifest that there had been a shift of balance in politics; ministers were becoming as fearful of the press as printers had been of high-handed persecution. "Let it be impressed upon your minds, let it be instilled into your children, that the liberty of the press is the *Palladium* of all the civil, political, and religious rights of an Englishman."[6] So "Junius" proclaimed in 1771, extolling a liberty that had not been so much as mentioned in the Bill of Rights of 1689, and was still to be established in formal legislation. With a command over readers, Junius and his like could cut a more dashing figure, present more extensive evidence, reach a more vast and lasting audience than any mere speaker in Parliament. And, protected by anonymity, such a writer could criticize more liberally, without fear of disgrace before even his closest neighbor. Ultimately, the press could circulate almost any man's thoughts, allowing them to rival those of any other man. Conversely, it could and did broadcast the errors, crimes, follies, and frailties of kings.

In London, this force was enhanced by peculiarities of geography. Court and Parliament were within sight of the City and its mobs, and the press could help stir up riots or fill the common streets with catchwords that penetrated noble sanctuaries. London also dominated the country as the central city, port, and capital of an island realm. In America, the force of the press was more diffuse in its immediate effects. There was no established national capital, and no national press, but a loose commerce among rival

[6] *The Letters of Junius*, ed. John Cannon (Oxford, 1978), p. 9.

cities and states along the coast and unsettled territories still to be developed inland. But from another angle the power of print was even more telling in these circumstances. How else, except through the press, could Americans come to understand themselves as citizens of a large and growing nation?

The problem implicitly presented to the Founders was how to replace old sanctions and authority with something momentous and enduring, yet comprehensible and immediate. The obvious method was warfare and conquest. Sovereignty was precisely understood as military control over an extent of territory. The Revolution bound Americans in a common cause, that of rejecting George III and his Parliament and redcoats in favor of local state assemblies, militias, and the Congress. In his second paper Publius could point to this achievement of national identity. "To all general purposes we have uniformly been one people—each individual citizen every where enjoying the same national rights, privileges, and protection. As a nation we have made peace and war—as a nation we have vanquished our common enemies—as a nation we have formed alliances and made treaties, and entered into various compacts and conventions with foreign States." But after a war where were citizens to observe their common institutions, especially if they were a people bred to distrust fortifications and standing armies? State governments were visible, but they were various and jealous of their own local powers. The national government under Confederation was less forceful and hence, to active patriots, it was an arrangement that was steadily proving inadequate.

What the Founders' generation did in effect was turn from conquest by force of arms to naturalization by force of debate. This was not a simple development, and not a matter of publications alone. It began in more personal forms, in Congress and state assemblies and in the contacts among their members. It continued through a cumbersome process of personal representation: delegates chosen warily by the states; plans and compromises at Annapolis and Philadelphia; campaigns, elections, and special conventions occurring in odd sequence from New Hampshire to Georgia. But what came forth and endured was a written constitution. The difference between states confederated under Congress, on the one hand, and the government of the United States, on the other, was a new printed document. It was common words—circulated, expounded, challenged, accepted, and established from one end of the country to another, and all within a very few months. The new government would still depend on military readiness; deliberations in a Congress would continue as the source of national laws. But the long ascent of the press as a political force here reached a new plateau. Without free publication the new form of government would have been impossible.

The Constitution and papers like the *Federalist*, in other words, should be understood as two aspects of the same historical change. The Constitution was drawn up to frame a government based on the assent of the people. The papers that had enlivened the American press from the 1760s onward were efforts to cultivate an informed public, a people who could give or withhold intelligent assent. And the *Federalist* encouraged such assent by drawing out common terms of discussion in several states, and preserving criticisms and full answers in a lasting volume.

Yet the closer one looks, the more evident it becomes that ratification took place in a special, and passing, climate of press freedom. This situation stands out in the confidentiality both of the Constitutional Convention and of the many debaters who published behind pseudonyms. If discussion had not been open, there could have been no debates worthy of the name, no free choice about a constitution, conceivably no constitution. But if discussion had been a shade freer we may also wonder about the consequences. Could there have been a productive session in Philadelphia, if each day's debates had been printed in the newspapers? Would criticism or defense have been as sharp and informative if every author wrote in his own name and was open to publicity about his private character and supposed motives? Within a few years the American press was to carry vigorous political journalism, conducted by both Republicans and Federalists. But this was not the case in 1787. The *Federalist* stands free of both personal and partisan distortions of this kind. Its form places it among the fully developed but still experimental efforts of eighteenth-century political rhetoric.

The result is a tone—and an authority—of high, privileged civility in debate. We have approached this tone already as a matter of candor. It is also a formality that seems to grow out of respectful tension between great assemblies and the press. We should bear in mind that many of the great political journalists of this time—from Addison and Wilkes to Hamilton and Madison—were also great figures in parliaments; there was no essential repugnance between these two forms of deliberation, aural and literate. A highly cultivated, well-prepared tone can be heard echoing from the parliaments and congresses of the late eighteenth and early nineteenth centuries, where educated gentlemen in power displayed their minds proudly, at full length, among their peers. And that tone carries further, into the press. For a while the same code of manners with which speakers addressed the honorable members of the opposition also affected published reports of their oratory. This was partly because of the dangers of libel or breach of privilege. But it could also be a matter of genuine, mutual respect. When Samuel Johnson evaded the laws by writing semifictitious debates of Parliament for the *Gentleman's Magazine* in the 1740s, he penned speeches that were long remembered as genuine—and magnificent.[7] And in the mid-nineteenth century, Walter Bagehot remarked acutely that a legislature, unlike a newspaper, could *act* to effect changes in public policy. "The great scene of debate," he wrote, "the great engine of popular instruction and political controversy, is the legislative assembly. A speech there by an eminent statesman, a party movement by a great political combination, are the best means yet known for arousing, enlivening, and teaching a people."[8] When newspapers were well enough established to report great speeches freely, they still had good reason for reporting them admiringly. Statesmen, in turn, had a further inducement to eloquence—the chance that their words would be overheard, recorded, and printed for wide and lasting fame.

A student of early American debates can hear this high civility running from colonial times down through Abraham Lincoln and Stephen Douglas. Many pages of the Virginia ratifying convention, with exchanges between Patrick Henry, George Mason, John Marshall, John Rutledge, and Madison read like the script of a dramatic pageant or the scenes from some lavish historical novel. The records of the Constitutional Convention in Philadelphia are less polished, but there too one can find ruffles and

[7] Arthur Murphy, *An Essay on the Life and Genius of Samuel Johnson* (1792) (rpt. in *Johnsonian Miscellanies*, ed. George Brikbeck Hill, 2 vols. [1897; rpt. London, 1966], I, 378–379); W. Jackson Bate, *Samuel Johnson* (New York, 1977), pp. 203–205.

[8] Walter Bagehot, *The English Constitution* (1867; rpt. London, 1963), p. 72.

flourishes (Hamilton's six-hour speech, Franklin's ceremonious remarks) as well as learned, penetrating disquisitions on the substantive issues.

And apart from tone, apart from the exercise of power, this legislative civility carries a definite authority. It represents reasoned agreement, a meeting of minds in a mood to hear, think, and act in concert. Actual assemblies may stray far from this ideal. But the legitimacy of modern legislation rests on its frequent attainment.

As we have seen, a strong argument running through the *Federalist* is that an uncanny harmony supported the deliberations in Philadelphia. Madison still cherished that memory nearly fifty years later. "I feel it a duty," he wrote, "to express my profound and solemn conviction, derived from my intimate opportunity of observing and appreciating the views of the Convention, collectively and individually, that there never was an assembly of men, charged with a great and arduous trust, who were more pure in their motives, or more exclusively or anxiously devoted to the object committed to them."[9] Thus he and many other delegates reinforced Publius's declarations that the Convention was a prodigy, and that the Constitution it produced was as good a work as could be produced by men in collaboration.

And the *Federalist* itself demonstrates this same authority. In its own time it had to be read as part of a national deliberation. It was papers answering other papers, risking tediousness in the name of full, informed discussion on the eve of momentous action. To a later time, this collection has emerged as collaborative in a different sense—as a rare merging of two or three distinctive American minds. In ei-

[9] Farrand, *Records*, III, 551.

ther light, the authority of Publius is strong because of his high civility.

That may seem odd, when set against the many press struggles of the eighteenth century and the cheapening of public debate by noisy publicity, then and later. But the form of the *Federalist* is, precisely, the form of eighteenth-century press freedom at its best.

CHAPTER FOUR

An Outcry against
Literate Civility

At the ratifying convention in Massachusetts, an older member stood up one morning to voice his objections. He told the delegates that he had been "on the stage in the beginning of our troubles, in the year 1775," and in those days such a constitution as the one before them would have been "thrown away at once." The Revolution had been fought over the unauthorized power to lay taxes, and now this new constitution would claim all the same rampant powers to take everything away from the states and the people.

> These lawyers, and men of learning, and moneyed men, that talk so finely, and gloss over matters so smoothly, to make us poor illiterate people swallow down the pill, expect to get into Congress themselves; they expect to be the managers of this Constitution, and get all the power and all the money into their own hands, and then they will swallow up all us little folks, like the great *Leviathan*, Mr. President; yes, just as

the whale swallowed up *Jonah*. This is what I am
afraid of.[1]

This little speech sums up a lot of antifederalist feeling.
It obviously carries an accent different from that found in
the published papers of New York and Philadelphia. It
speaks with a voice of personal urgency and outrage, the
voice of one Amos Singletary, who had fought a revolution for clear principles and now feared the loss of his liberties in a new contrivance of fancy words and national powers. Perhaps its loudest message is fear—fear of a kind that
is almost unanswerable. If Singletary and others saw all
proponents of the Constitution as smooth-talking trick-
sters, then there is no way that they could see any literate
man as honest or reliable. Literacy and chicanery are united,
lumped together as a "they" who are essentially in league
against "all us little folks," out to "make all us poor illiterate people swallow down the pill." Yet there is something
that rings true in these lines, an ancient grudge of rural folk
against doctors and lawyers they have reasons to distrust.
And the passage as a whole could be aimed keenly at the
heart of the *Federalist*. For there a lawyer (Hamilton) and a
man of learning (Madison), moneyed men both, did talk
very finely and did expect to get into power themselves
and be managers of the new constitution.

A shrewd little farmer here, a few score miles away from
the bigger cities and their newspapers, seems to see through
Publius and all his pomps. How can he be answered?

[1] Jonathan Elliot, ed., *The Debates of the Several State Conventions on
the Adoption of the Federal Constitution*, 2d ed., 5 vols. (Philadelphia,
1861), II, 101–102. These Massachusetts debates were reported widely
at the time. Singletary's speech and Smith's reply appeared in the *New-
York Journal*, March 11 and 12, 1788.

A Vocal Answer

As it happened, this particular speaker was answered very fully, in his own language and on his own ground. The next speaker at that convention, on February 25, 1788, was another obscure farmer, a plain "Honorable Mr. Smith," Jonathan Smith of Berkshire County. "Mr. President," he began, "I am a plain man, and get my living by the plough. I am not used to speak in public, but I beg your leave to say a few words to my brother ploughjoggers in this house." He had seen anarchy in Shays's Rebellion of 1786 in his part of the state, and he wanted to remind his brother farmers that the common people, when lawless, could be a terrifying mob.

> People I say took up arms; and then, if you went to speak to them, you had the musket of death presented to your breast. They would rob you of your property; threaten to burn your houses; oblige you to be on your guard night and day; alarms spread from town to town; families were broken up; the tender mother would cry, "O, my son is among them! What shall I do for my child!" Some were taken captive, children taken out of their schools, and carried away. Then we should hear of an action, and the poor prisoners were set in the front, to be killed by their own friends. How dreadful, how distressing was this! Our distress was so great that we should have been glad to snatch at any thing that looked like a government. Had any person, that was able to protect us, come and set up his standard, we should all have flocked to it, even if it had been a monarch; and that monarch might have proved a tyrant;—so that you see that anarchy leads to tyranny, and better have one tyrant than so many at once.

Here Smith seems to be confirming Singletary's worst fears—that a new generation could prefer even monarchy to popular liberty. But in his next paragraph Smith squarely prefers the new constitution as "a cure for these disorders."

> I got a copy of it, and read it over and over. I had been a member of the Convention to form our own state constitution, and had learnt something of the checks and balances of power, and I found them all here. I did not go to any lawyer, to ask his opinion; we have no lawyers in our town, and we do well enough without. I formed my own opinion, and was pleased with this Constitution. My honorable old daddy there [pointing to Mr. Singletary] won't think that I expect to be a Congress-man, and swallow up the liberties of the people. I never had any post, nor do I want one. But I don't think the worse of the Constitution because lawyers, and men of learning, and moneyed men, are fond of it. I don't suspect that they want to get into Congress and abuse their power. I am not of such a jealous make. They that are honest men themselves are not apt to suspect other people. I don't know why our constituents have not a good right to be as jealous of us as we seem to be of the Congress; and I think those gentlemen, who are so very suspicious that as soon as a man gets into power he turns rogue, had better look at home.
>
> [Elliot, *Debates*, ii, 102–103]

These speeches may have been touched up by the literate gentleman who recorded them, but they still show their own power. Smith gives Singletary an effectual answer. The older man had said that he might have more to say later, but in fact he never rose again in these debates. Moreover, Smith has a very deep, experiential sense of constitutional government. Without law or authority of some kind, men turn to riot. As an escape from that, they may accept any form of authority, even tyranny. But a written constitution offers another way out, and the fact that it is written does not necessarily make it inscrutable or a device for usurpation. Mr. Smith catches Mr. Singletary in a delicate position: he himself has been speaking in a forum for privileged, civilized debate; his own state derives liberties from a written constitution; all good government rests on some kind of trust. Here, far from Publius, is another voice urging civility and candor, though in homely words that even call another legislator "my honorable old daddy there."

Untenable Assumptions

Looking back on the ratification debates, we can also remark that Singletary's fear of literacy was an anachronism. By the eighteenth century, law in the English-speaking world was published law. In America the only imaginable means of establishing a government was by charters, constitutions, formally articulated agreements. There were rumors in the summer of 1787 that the Philadelphia Convention was contemplating a return to personal government. Hamilton spent some effort tracing the source of a notion that Frederick, duke of York, was to be invited to ascend an American throne.[2] But even these wild rumors depended on circulation by letter and newspaper; they took most of their force from the fact that the deliberations

[2] Hamilton to Jeremiah Wadsworth, August 20, 1787, in *The Papers of Alexander Hamilton*, ed. Harold C. Syrett and Jacob E. Cooke, 24 vols. (New York, 1961–1979), IV, 236.

in Philadelphia were going on in secret—that is, were *not* immediately publishable.

There is also something in Singletary's speech that borders on disingenuousness. There is a ploy of the demagogue, which asserts that the people—or the "real" people, or "we, the people"—are essentially the poor, the illiterate, and the oppressed. But the leader who makes this assertion will always tacitly and maybe unwittingly except himself. He must. To be a leader he has to exercise power, be articulate, and see through oppression. This assertion he makes has a superficial appeal; it seems to be all-embracing, democratic, Christian, widely tolerant and sympathetic toward the masses. It recognizes that most men, women, and children do not become political leaders; that many are incapacitated for government; and yet that all deserve certain rights and respect in the human community. It is a pernicious notion, nonetheless. It is inherently demeaning to any society. It implies that its citizens are finally unworthy of respect, and that any assent drawn from them is uninformed and only a shade away from coercion. Furthermore, it hampers the development of strong and wise statesmanship by casting suspicion on free clashes of intellect. It makes candidacy for office rest on birth in a log cabin, vigorous sportsmanship, or other appearances of good fellowship, rather than on refinements or distinction of mind in the public forum. Folksy appearances may have reinforced the strengths of a Lincoln, but the lack of them seems to have crippled Wilson and would disqualify a latterday Washington, Adams, Jefferson, Madison, Hamilton, Jay, Rush, or Gouverneur Morris.

Singletary's speech is not addressed to the people at large; it seems honestly to express a small man's fears in a great assembly. But it does contain an unconscious sign of false posing. Singletary may have been the semiliterate representative of a largely illiterate constituency.[3] But like many a New Englander, he had reams of book learning at his fingers' ends and town-meeting tactics running in his veins. His closing is the giveaway: "They will swallow up all us little folks, like the great *Leviathan*, Mr. President; yes, just as the whale swallowed up *Jonah*." There is a practiced speaker behind these rhythms and a well-thumbed Bible behind the allusions. Jonathan Smith is quite alert to these nuances, in his reply. Smith does not present himself as illiterate (he got the new constitution "and read it over and over"), although he does introduce himself as a humble ploughjogger. And when he comes to his close, he matches the Book of Jonah with the Book of Ecclesiastes. "Some gentlemen say, Don't be in a hurry; take time to consider, and don't take a leap in the dark. I say, Take things in time; gather fruit when it is ripe. There is a time to sow and a time to reap; we sowed our seed when we sent men to the federal Convention; now is the harvest, now is the time to reap the fruit of our labor; and if we don't do it now, I am afraid we never shall have another opportunity."[4]

[3] According to the surviving records, Singletary (1721–1806) was the first male child born in the town of Sutton, Massachusetts, near Worcester. He never went to school, but picked up the rudiments of learning at home; yet he became distinguished as a representative in state assemblies and as a local justice of the peace. He and his wife seem to have been converted to earnest Christianity by the preaching of Jonathan Edwards in Sutton in 1742. See William A. Benedict and Hiram A. Tracy, *History of the Town of Sutton, Massachusetts, from 1704 to 1876* (Worcester, Mass., 1878), pp. 726–728. Much less seems to be known about Jonathan Smith, apart from the fact that he represented Lanesborough and that Elliot's *Debates* wrongly record him as voting against the Constitution. See Samuel Bannister Harding, *The Contest over the Ratification of the Federal Constitution in the State of Massachusetts*, Harvard Historical Studies, vol. 2 (New York, 1896), pp. 77–78.

[4] Elliot, *Debates*, II, 104. This passage may also refine a familiar prov-

Unanswerable Language, Unshakable Doubt

Both these speeches, however, imply a deep criticism of the *Federalist*; for literate or not, these are speeches that can be heard. They carry a human voice. They are the open utterances of identifiable speakers. Their phrases stick in the memory, sometimes word for word. They have a force next to which many of Publius's efforts look paper-thin.

These speakers know how to lay hold of the imagination. Their language is simple, direct, vital, immediate. "They will swallow up all us little folks." "People I say took up arms; and then, if you went to speak to them, you had the musket of death presented to your breast." Standing right before their audiences, both Singletary and Smith know how to reach for their ears. They can tell a story, turn a phrase, give a commonplace idea the sharpness of metaphor and the urgency of rhythm.

Publius makes a very different form of address. He expects his reader to take his time, weigh propositions and abstractions, follow a long development of related ideas, compare one passage with another. There are a few places where Publius rises to eloquence and takes on a speaking voice. But for the most part he requires a reader bent over a page, a reader experienced with other long arguments and prepared to read some involved sentences, and reread them if necessary, in order to arrive at a precise understanding.

In short, Publius appeals to literacy of a particular kind. Singletary is wrong to suspect literacy in any form, but he is right to detect that the Constitution and its greatest de-

---

erb from Samuel Butler's *Hudibras*, Part 2, Canto 2, lines 501–503:

> Have a care o' th' main chance
> And look before you ere you leap;
> For, as you sow, you are like to reap.

fenders were developing a new departure in government. They were assuming that government could now rest on a citizenry of the prosperous, the very literate, and the free. They were setting up expectations that national politicians would be bookish men, at least as familiar with abstract thought as they were with the needs and life patterns of their homely neighbors. This assumption contains a very real threat to men like Singletary. Immediately, it was to mean that national politics would be different in kind from the personal acquaintance between voters and their local officials. In the long run, it threatened a deeper parting of the ways. A new generation would have to gain from books what earlier men gained from direct experience. If they could not master such learning, their institutions would be beyond them.

This, I think, is why Singletary's outcry can be effectively refuted and yet come back to touch an exposed nerve in American life. Singletary was aware of certain rhythms in life—rhythms that the Constitution and most of its discussants deliberately ignored. To countless generations, the constitution of government had been a matter of unalterable fact, like the heights of the hills or the changes of the seasons. Now a new document was presented for ratification, purporting to make the constitution a matter of choice, of reason and will. To one cast of mind, retained by many an antifederalist, the constitution was an account of the way things were, of institutions worked out through time—like the state governments and Articles of Confederation. To another cast of mind, the constitution was a description of what America should become—even at the cost of abandoning ingrained ways.

The difference lay in an act of faith or daring. Publius opened with a solemn sense of this impending choice, as we have already noted. In the final number of the *Federalist* he came back to the same point. He quoted one of Hume's essays: "To balance a large state or society . . . is a work of so great difficulty, that no human genius, however comprehensive, is able by the mere dint of reason and reflection, to effect it. The judgments of many must unite in the work: EXPERIENCE must guide their labour: TIME must bring it to perfection: And the FEELING of inconveniences must correct the mistakes which they *inevitably* fall into, in their first trials and experiments." At this point seven states had ratified the Constitution and Publius is here warning against tampering or conditional ratification by the remaining conventions, including New York's. But experience, time, and feeling still mean what they mean. Publius goes on to say in his own words what he often said throughout these papers: "The establishment of a constitution, in time of profound peace, by the voluntary consent of a whole people, is a PRODIGY, to the completion of which I look forward with trembling anxiety." Thereafter—*after* the completion of ratification, *after* the establishment of a strong national government—time, experience, and feeling could do their work of reconciling a new pattern to the needs of a growing nation. For now, the issue was whether the prodigy would occur at all, "whether societies of men are really capable or not, of establishing good government from reflection and choice" (No. 1).

Singletary gives voice to a lasting doubt. What he says is not intellectual; it would be much easier to answer if it were. Instead it is a feeling in the bones. Singletary had risen a few days earlier in the Massachusetts convention, to speak on another issue. His words may look flat on the page, but they carry another heavy load of implication.

The Hon. Mr. Singletary thought we were giving up all our privileges, as there was no provision that men

in power should have any *religion*; and though he
hoped to see Christians, yet, by the Constitution, a
Papist, or an Infidel, was as eligible as they. It had
been said that men had not degenerated; he did not
think men were better now than when men after God's
own heart did wickedly. He thought, in this instance,
we were giving great power to we know not whom.

[Elliot, *Debates*, II, 44]

To a modern eye this passage looks quaint if not reaction-
ary, a throwback to religious test acts for officeholders. But
from a believer in Massachusetts, speaking in an assembly
that had just come from attending morning prayers, such a
speech would not be odd. Many states had long known a
close connection between church and government. The
Massachusetts Bill of Rights (1780) still specified that it
was the "right as well as the duty of all men . . . to worship the Supreme Being"; that the legislature should provide for "the public worship of God and the support and
maintenance of public Protestant teachers of piety, religion, and morality"; and that the legislature had "authority
to enjoin upon all subjects an attendance upon the instruc-
tions of the public teachers aforesaid."[5] Jefferson fought
such a hard battle to separate church and state in Virginia
that he listed the Statute of Religious Liberty (1786) as one
of the three great accomplishments of his life. To many
men the power of government could not be a matter of
pure reflection and choice. Like all other powers on earth,
it derived from God.

"He did not think men were better now than when men
after God's own heart did wickedly." Here, too, Singletary
is referring to Scripture, to the line in which the prophet
Samuel reproves Saul and notifies him that a new king,

[5] Massachusetts Bill of Rights, in *Documents of American History*, ed.
Henry Steele Commager, 9th ed. (New York, 1973), pp. 107–108.

David, will take his place: "But now thy kingdom shall not continue: the Lord hath sought him a man after his own heart, and the Lord hath commanded him to be captain over his people, because thou hast not kept that which the Lord commanded thee" (1 Samuel 13:14). David also did wickedly when he came to power, and suffered God's punishment as a result. Singletary is clearly recalling that these were the original biblical kings, military heroes granted to the people by God and endowed with great powers, but still men who were insufficient by themselves. Though he does not say it openly, his allusion says it for him: the new, wholly secular constitution, which was creating great powers for national taxation and military action, could be a long step toward the worship of Baal.[6]

Of course, some such step was occurring anyhow. As we have already seen, the meaning of the constitution was changing in the eighteenth century, in Europe as well as America. Divine prerogatives of kingship could not withstand the Enlightenment. Singletary's own familiarity with Scripture rested on the widespread publishing of bibles and the encouragement of popular education, so that common men could read and judge even things divine for themselves. Carried to its logical extreme, Singletary's position is again untenable. He is yearning for the restraints of a common faith, while speaking out almost

---

[6] Singletary's speech also recalls an exchange that took place two days earlier. A Reverend Mr. West argued that the men chosen to administer the new government would be, in general, good men. Another speaker rose and replied that he was surprised at such language from a clergyman. "When I consider the man that slew the lion and the bear, and that he was a man after *God's own heart*—when I consider his son, blessed with *all wisdom*, and the errors they fell into,—I extremely doubt the infallibility of human nature" (Elliot, *Debates*, II, 33–34). A similar biblical allusion appeared in the *New-York Morning-Post* for December 1, 1787, where a correspondent contributed 1 Samuel 8—Samuel's dire warning of a mortal king's powers of conscription and taxation—as an argument against the Constitution.

alone in a modern ratifying convention.

But can a government rest on pure reflection and choice? That question remains even after the speaker and all his idiosyncracies have long since perished. The Bible accounts for creation, temptation, captivity, deliverance, catastrophe, miracle. Its enduring authority embraces centuries of common people's understanding of these forces beyond human control. Its poetry harmonizes personal and societal experiences of ultimate good and ultimate evil. Parables of common laborers are blended with the songs of great kings and the visions of prophets. Against this richness of Western civilization, deepened by centuries of European art, literature, music, and architecture, of what weight are the pages of the *Federalist* or the articulated experiences of one generation living along the Atlantic seaboard between 1763 and 1789?

After two centuries these questions remain unanswered. Millions of Singletaries have found the Constitution and the modern state barren substitutes for the felt realities of a living religious heritage. The doubters have included some great American thinkers, and not all of them have been religious conservatives.

> Faun's flesh is not to us,
> Nor the saint's vision.
> We have the press for wafer;
> Franchise for circumcision.[7]

So the figure in Ezra Pound's "Hugh Selwyn Mauberly" sings bitterly early in this century; and his echoes are still in the air. At the opposite extreme are the millions who

[7] Ezra Pound, *Personae*, p. 189. Copyright 1926 by Ezra Pound. Reprinted by permission of New Directions Publishing Corporation and Faber and Faber Ltd.

have turned to the American Constitution as the source of a common faith, who continue to see it as the central instrument of modern human liberation. The controversy between Smith and Singletary, between federalist and antifederalist, between the *Federalist* and the townsfolk of New England has become an ongoing dialogue, never resolved and never to be resolved by any mere vote or rational demonstration.

Singletary's odd voice thus marks the limit of the authority of Publius. As a literate, civil, rational spokesman for modernity (though in the guise, or at least the name, of an ancient sage), Publius cannot move some loyalties. He cannot counter or satisfy some human longings. It would be idle to wonder how a full-blown, spiritually satisfying constitution might have emerged in the 1780s, harmonized by an American Milton. The nature of the American experience was to begin anew, try an experiment, cast off crown and pulpit by calling upon modern newspaper prose to justify a new departure. The poetry of such a changed world would have to emerge, as No. 85 admits, through experience, time, and feeling. But the first large step is bare law, devoid of the graces of imagery, softened only by long deliberation and free discussion, and opening a dangerous discontinuity between old authorities and new.

CHAPTER FIVE

Shifting Contexts of
Federalist No. 10

To thousands if not millions of readers, the modern authority of the *Federalist* is concentrated in one paper, No. 10. This is the *Federalist* essay most often anthologized, taught, studied, and remembered in this century. It appears in introductory textbooks of history, rhetoric, American literature, and political science. From time to time it appears or is quoted on editorial pages, and every autumn an army of college professors must expound it. It is an appealing example of formal reasoning, for it moves from clear definitions and straightforward propositions to a remarkable conclusion about the function of parties and interest groups in a large society. Its few hundred words demand close attention but repay it with a seminal idea about political life. The paper seems to be a compact sample of the *Federalist* at its best, a work of seemingly unanswerable logic in defense of the Constitution. It leaves a strong impression that Hamilton and Madison framed and argued about the foundations of government with uncanny lucidity and penetration.

The longer one looks at this paper, however, the more

puzzling it becomes. Usually one can study a famous speech or essay and make certain very safe statements about who wrote it, on what occasion, and in relation to what other, similar works. This framework then supports a very exact search for its meaning. I suppose that in this case many teachers state flatly that this paper was written by Madison to encourage ratification and to answer the commonplace antifederalist objection that republican government could never work in a large country. But a little homework will also reveal that this paper appears right next to a similar paper claimed by Hamilton. The professor may know that No. 10 addresses not only antifederalists and their writings but also some pages from Montesquieu, and that it borrows a central idea and some precise terms from the writings of David Hume. By now the reader of this book may be convinced of the composite nature of *Federalist* authorship and the intricate implications of essays in a newspaper series. There are other considerations that one should weigh, too, including the origins and later uses of this argument and the recent history of No. 10 as the keystone paper of the whole set. In short, a conscientious reader has to recognize that this paper reprinted by itself is an argument presented out of context. What is worse, it is an argument that seems self-contained but is actually torn from a multitude of contexts. All of these circumstantial details affect the way the paper can be interpreted; many of them clash with one another; none can be established as the primary clue to its meaning. Every single approach leads to a reading that is evidently incomplete, and in the end this paper cannot bear the weight that most readers want to ascribe to it.

At this point one may be tempted to draw a line. The simplest and most sensible course is to read and reread the *Federalist* as a whole, understanding that each of its segments is indissolubly bonded to the others and that the design of the entire series is what matters. But that approach will not quite do, either. Most of the papers appeared on separate dates, as separate, integral essays. Each one invites a complex reading, as both a single essay and an installment in the series.

Candor thus urges us forward, to review No. 10 in all its contexts, and to evaluate them as well as we can. This paper may present some special difficulties, but then so may any single *Federalist* under close scrutiny. This one will serve as a fair sample of the complexity of Publius's thought, and because of its great celebrity it will reveal a curious turn in these papers' authority in recent years.

An Exemplary Argument

The tenth *Federalist* first came out on November 22, 1787. It appeared by itself in the *Daily Advertiser*, a newspaper that had not given first publication to any earlier number, and from its first words it seems to stand apart as a compact essay on a single topic. It opens with a full statement of the difficulties that factions throw in the way of good government. "Among the numerous advantages promised by a well constructed Union, none deserves to be more accurately developed than its tendency to break and control the violence of faction." Publius then supplies a definition of his most important term. "By a faction I understand a number of citizens, whether amounting to a majority or minority of the whole, who are united and actuated by some common impulse of passion, or of interest, adverse to the rights of other citizens, or to the permanent and aggregate interests of the community." One might quarrel with the bland assumption of clear meaning for some of these terms. What exactly does the author have in mind by the "rights" that a faction should not violate? Or how are the "permanent and aggregate interests" of a society ever to be decided, particularly in a new, large, and growing country? But on the whole this definition provides a forthright, considered starting point. With this general term fixed in this way, Publius proceeds through a series of alternative propositions, rejecting some, approving others, until he arrives at a proof that a large, strong union provides a cure for the evils of faction.

There are two ways, he states, of curing the mischiefs of faction: "the one, by removing its causes; the other, by controling its effects." Turning immediately to ways of removing causes, Publius names two further alternatives: removing liberty, or developing the same opinions, passions, and interests in every citizen. The first is intolerable; the second is impossible. In a republican society liberty is essential to political life; and judges, legislators, and the most enlightened statesmen will be powerless to escape clashing interests that are sown in the nature of man. Thus causes of faction cannot be removed; its evils must be addressed by controlling its effects.

On this topic Publius again looks at pairs of alternatives. If the faction is a minority, its evils will be limited by majority rule; if a faction is a majority, however, it can run out of control. To obtain relief, only two means are available. "Either the existence of the same passion or interest in a majority at the same time, must be prevented; or the majority, having such co-existent passion or interest, must be rendered, by their number and situation, unable to concert and carry into effect schemes of oppression."

At this point, a further distinction of alternatives emerges, which clarifies the worst and best developments of both these means of control. The worst case is pure democracy; the best is good republican government. "A pure Democracy, by which I mean, a Society, consisting of a small number of citizens, who assemble and administer the Government in person, can admit of no cure for the mischiefs of faction." Common passions will always sway large crowds and the means to carry them into effect will always be available to majorities. But a republic, "by which I mean a Government in which the scheme of representation takes place," offers a cure for faction. Again, there are two large reasons for this.

The first is that the government is delegated to representatives of the people. This delegation could have two effects. It could work to "refine and enlarge the public views, by passing them through the medium of a chosen body of citizens, whose wisdom may best discern the true interest of their country, and whose patriotism and love of justice, will be least likely to sacrifice it to temporary or partial considerations." But there is also the danger that representatives could pervert a government, gain control only to serve their own ends and betray the people.

Thus the second advantage of representative government stands out: it can involve a large number of citizens over a "greater sphere of country." Again, this advantage has two aspects. First, a larger territory and population offer a greater likelihood of worthy characters as candidates for office; and since representatives will be chosen from larger constituencies, there is less likelihood of corrupt electioneering. Second, a great extent of territory makes it almost impossible for a national majority to emerge and act effectively. "Extend the sphere, and you take in a greater variety of parties and interests; you make it less probable that a majority of the whole will have a common motive to invade the rights of other citizens; or if such a common motive exists, it will be more difficult for all who feel it to discover their own strength, and to act in unison with each other."

These points are the core of the doctrine of *Federalist* No. 10. Publius has only to make one last turn and declare that good republican government will be achieved in union under the Constitution. "Hence it clearly appears, that the same advantage, which a Republic has over a Democracy, in controling the effects of faction, is enjoyed by a large over a small Republic—is enjoyed by the Union over the States composing it." He then reviews these advantages in detail and concludes very neatly. "In the extent and proper structure of the Union, therefore, we behold a Republican remedy for the diseases most incident to Republican Government. And according to the degree of pleasure and pride, we feel in being Republicans, ought to be our zeal in cherishing the spirit, and supporting the character of Federalists."

No summary can capture the full detail of this essay or the deft precision with which abstract reasoning about faction is united with steady pressure in favor of Constitutional federalism. But this summary should make clear that this paper deserves the close study it usually gets. Its terms and development are so lucid, and its subject is so central to theories of modern government, that almost every phrase stands out. One may quarrel with details or notice further points that deserve greater stress, but that is because every element of the paper is so carefully wrought. The binary progression of logic seems to lead inexorably to the final point. Choose This or That; since This is impossible, then That—or more precisely, That A or That B; and since That A is intolerable, then That B. At each step a possible alternative has to be firmly rejected, and at the end there is no going back. The extinction of liberty, the imposition of common motives and passions, and the dangers of majority rule in a pure democracy or small republic have all been examined and set aside. What is left is republican government, union, a federal system, a large country, a cure for faction—and the conviction that the citizens who have adopted the American Constitution have had the benefit of a rare, clearsighted understanding of their choices.

As it stands now, the most famous and widely read paper in the *Federalist*, this essay is one of the finest brief, open civics lessons in history. That claim can be made without irony. The paper simultaneously defines, celebrates, and changes the political awareness of a great people. And it succinctly sets out the key terms of a modern political problem. Its analysis may be inadequate or mistaken in the end; but the paper presents a case that has to be understood and met by anyone who would explain the best workings of factions in a free society.

Madison and Publius

Both Hamilton and Madison agreed in assigning the authorship of this paper to Madison. It thus appears as Madison's first contribution to the *Federalist*. Other versions of the argument can also be found in Madison's writings of this period, and in some of the later *Federalists* ascribed to him. But for reasons we have already surveyed, it is hard to ascribe any paper in the *Federalist* to a single author. Madison surely had a strong interest in the materials of this paper. He may have composed its final draft. But in it we must also see the merging of Madison with Publius. The paper is different from what Madison wrote elsewhere, and the differences matter.

Madison had earlier discussed the theory of faction and republican government in four places: a memorandum he prepared for the Constitutional Convention, two speeches he gave there, and a letter to Thomas Jefferson. Exact repetitions of ideas and phrases show that the material in No. 10 underwent a process of refinement between the spring of 1787 and November, that is from preliminary notes to participation in the Convention, to reconsideration after its close, to publication in the *Federalist*. The central idea also changed in two important ways.

First, the idea that extended republican government was a sufficient cure for the evils of faction emerged only in No. 10. Earlier Madison held that the extended republic was one possible answer to the tyranny of the majority. It appeared along with other remedies, which were understood as distinct from and sometimes quite contrary to it. The doctrine of the extended republic appears in the memorandum "Vices of the Political System of the United States," under "Injustice of the laws of the States," the eleventh of twelve faults Madison listed.

> If an enlargement of the sphere is found to lessen the insecurity of private rights, it is not because the impulse of a common interest or passion is less predominant in this case with the majority; but because a common interest or passion is less apt to be felt and the requisite combinations less easy to be formed by a great than by a small number. The Society becomes broken into a greater variety of interests, of pursuits, of passions, which check each other, whilst those who may feel a common sentiment have less opportunity of communication and concert. It may be inferred that

[119]

the inconveniences of popular States contrary to the prevailing Theory, are in proportion not to the extent, but to the narrowness of their limits.[1]

This is much sketchier and cruder than the *Federalist* version; and another check on unjust laws is presented a paragraph later—a cumbersome addition in cumbersome language.

> An auxiliary desideratum for the melioration of the Republican form is such a process of elections as will most certainly extract from the mass of Society the purest and noblest characters which it contains; such as will at once feel most strongly the proper motives to pursue the end of their appointment, and be most capable to devise the proper means of attaining it. [*PJM*, IX, 357]

At the Constitutional Convention, Madison presented his theory in conjunction with other schemes. On June 6 he stated that "the only remedy" for majority faction was "to enlarge the sphere, & thereby divide the community." But later that same day he spoke up in favor of his other great doctrine for the preservation of minority rights, a national power to veto state legislation (*PJM*, X, 33, 35–36). On June 26 he spoke on elections and qualifications for the Senate. Here he raised a new problem of majority rule: a growth of population leading to the rise of a great majority "of those who will labor under all the hardships of life, & secretly sigh for a more equal distribution of its blessings." To guard against agrarian revolution, Madison advocated a Senate drawn from the "opulent minority," men advanced

---

[1] *The Papers of James Madison*, ed. Robert A. Rutland et al., IX (Chicago, 1975), 356–357 (hereafter cited as *PJM*).

in age and made secure with long terms of office (*PJM*, x, 77–78).

After the Convention had modified or rejected many of these ideas, Madison wrote out his private reflections for Jefferson in a letter of October 24. In a long discussion of republican government, he presented his idea of a sphere large enough to check an unjust majority. But he still felt that a negative on state laws was necessary to stable government. And concerning the size of a republican government, he had a second thought: "It must be observed however that this doctrine can only hold within a sphere of mean extent. As in too small a sphere oppressive combinations may be too easily formed agst. the weaker party; so in too extensive a one, a defensive concert may be rendered too difficult against the oppression of those entrusted with the administration." The new government of the United States would benefit, he concluded, not only from large territory and population, but also from the newly developed balance between state and federal powers (*PJM*, x, 214).

The second change in the central idea of the tenth *Federalist* was its very tight schematic presentation. In its earlier forms, the enlarged-sphere doctrine appears as a discursive observation, a theoretic point which strengthens other lines of argument. In No. 10, all other ideas converge to the development of this theory and its significance for the union. In fact, other ideas that Madison had dealt with alongside this one are here incorporated into it. The choice of wise and prudent representatives is made a consequence, not a supplement, of enlarging the sphere. Republican principles and federal principles are presented as identical, not coincidental.

It may be thought that Madison followed a very ordinary development here, and revised his ideas during a year

of debate and reflection until they reached their most polished form when he wrote for publication. But the process
of reconsideration also continued beyond that point. In
later *Federalist* papers, the ideas of No. 10 are extended and
qualifed so that much of its compact force is loosened and
undone.

Paper No. 14, claimed by Madison, discusses the extent
of the union and defends the idea that republican government can thrive in such a large territory. But it also makes
several further points. The federal government will be limited to certain enumerated powers; the full republic will
change its dimensions through time, as new states join the
union and internal communications are improved; almost
every state will border on a frontier (the Atlantic, Canada,
the unsettled West), so that states far from the seat of federal power will have a strong inducement to support national government and rely on it for defense. All of these
observations support the idea of union, but not all of them
strengthen the ideal theory of republican government in a
large but stable society.

Paper No. 51, also claimed by Madison, reviews several
checks on tyranny in the new government. The last is the
central republican doctrine: "Whilst all authority . . . will
be derived from and dependent on the society, the society
itself will be broken into so many parts, interests and
classes of citizens, that the rights of individuals or of the
minority, will be in little danger from interested combinations of the majority." This idea is also celebrated at the
end of the paper. "In the extended republic of the United
States, and among the great variety of interests, parties and
sects which it embraces, a coalition of a majority of the
whole society could seldom take place on any other principles than those of justice and the general good." But in the
course of this paper, Publius reviews two other ways of

limiting centralized power. One is the separation of powers, including the division of legislative power between the
House and the Senate. The other is the division of power
between state and federal governments. The final sentence
of this paper seems to echo the conclusion of No. 10, with
its identification of republicanism and federalism. But there
is a difference. The language Publius uses is burdened with
these further ideas at this point, and the great theory is di-
luted if not muddied by them. "Happily for the *republican
cause*, the practicable sphere may be carried to a very great
extent, by a judicious modification and mixture of the *federal principle*."

Paper No. 63, claimed by Madison as his final contribution to the series, returns to the theory of the enlarged
sphere, in relation to the importance of the Senate. Publius
argues that such a body of temperate and respectable citizens may check the people themselves from rushing head-
long into measures they will later regret. He recalls his earlier words: "It may be suggested that a people spread over
an extensive region, cannot like the crouded inhabitants of
a small district, be subject to the infection of violent passions; or to the danger of combining in the pursuit of
unjust measures. I am far from denying that this is a distinction of peculiar importance. I have on the contrary en-
deavoured in a former paper, to shew that it is one of the
principal recommendations of a confederated republic."
But here he turns sharply away from this theory. "At the
same time this advantage ought not to be considered as su-
perseding the use of auxiliary precautions." The next sentence turns the celebrated theory on its head. "It may even
be remarked that the same extended situation which will
exempt the people of America from some of the dangers
incident to lesser republics, will expose them to the incon-
veniency of remaining for a longer time, under the in-

fluence of those misrepresentations which the combined industry of interested men may succeed in distributing among them." In other words, unjust majority rule remains a possibility in a republic. What is worse, the fragmentation of society in a large republic makes it harder to overturn an unjust government, if it ever does come to power!

Beyond the *Federalist* it is difficult to trace Madison's thought on large republics. There is no further celebrated pronouncement that would link his name to ideas like those in No. 10. He seems to have dropped the subject once the *Federalist* was in print, the Constitution was adopted, and his efforts were devoted to the practical issues of governing. But from what we can see here, his thoughts never did reach a satisfying clarity. *Federalist* No. 10 by itself seems definitive. Set against Madison's fluid ponderings of the same ideas, it becomes a different thing. If the theory is attributed to Madison, we must ask which Madison, or Madison at which point in his continuous reconsiderations. If the theory is more rightly the property of Publius, it still is entangled in ambiguities from one paper to another.

Publius and Hamilton

No one has ever claimed that Hamilton wrote the tenth *Federalist*, but the ideas in that paper also appear in some of his writings. If we consider that he planned the opening strategies of the series, we can also see his hand in the shape of its rigorous argument.

Hamilton's notes show that he was listening carefully when Madison first broached the theory of large republican government in the Convention. He kept rough notes and added reflections of his own. His very first such jotting, for June 1, 1787, has an astonishing ring: "The way to prevent a majority from having an interest to oppress the minority is to enlarge the sphere."[2] When Madison discussed this theory on June 6, Hamilton again recorded the main principles, then wrote out a brief critique. Both enlarged territory and refined representation, Hamilton agreed, were true principles on which republics should be constructed—"but they do not conclude so strongly as he supposes."

> The Assembly when chosen will meet in one room if they are drawn from half the globe—& will be liable to all the passions of popular assemblies.
> If more *minute links* are wanting others will supply them. Distinctions of Eastern middle and Southern states will come into view; between commercial and non commercial states. Imaginary lines will influence &c. Human mind prone to limit its view by near & local objects. Paper money is capable of giving a general impulse. It is easy to conceive a popular sentiment pervading the E[astern] states.   [*PAH*, IV, 165]

To Madison's suggestion that large districts are less liable to be influenced by factions or demagogues, Hamilton also had a ready response.

> This is in some degree true but not so generally as may be supposed. Frequently small portions of the large districts carry elections. An influential demagogue will give an impulse to the whole. Demagogues are not always *inconsiderable* persons. Patricians were frequently demagogues. Characters are less known & a less active interest taken in them.   [*PAH*, x, 166]

[2] *The Papers of Alexander Hamilton*, ed. Harold C. Syrett and Jacob E. Cooke, 24 vols. (New York, 1961–79), IV, 161 (hereafter cited as *PAH*).

It is not necessary to work out exactly what Hamilton meant in some of these cryptic jottings. What stands out is that Madison's idea was percolating in Hamilton's mind, too. It caught his attention; it provoked him to scribble down the heads of a rejoinder; it stuck in his memory.

When he came to the *Federalist*, he was prepared to develop such notions himself. Just before No. 10 stands a paper, claimed by Hamilton, in which Publius traces other advantages of enlarging the sphere. *Federalist* No. 9 reviews the turbulence of faction and revolution in earlier republics, and draws comfort from several great improvements in the science of politics. Modern republican governments rely on legislative checks and balances, judicial tenure during good behavior, and popular elections of representatives. Publius now offers a fourth principle, one "which has been made the foundation of an objection to the New Constitution, I mean the ENLARGEMENT of the ORBIT within which such systems are to revolve either in respect to the dimensions of a single State, or to the consolidation of several smaller States into one great confederacy."

This link between Nos. 9 and 10 has been noticed for years, at least since John Quincy Adams referred to it in his eulogy for Madison in 1836.[3] But it has usually been used to point a contrast between the two *Federalist* authors: Hamilton the nationalist argues for national power to quell local uprisings in No. 9; Madison the libertarian explores the more republican remedy for faction in No. 10. In fact, these two papers are very closely harmonized; No. 9 prepares the way for No. 10. "Referring the examination of

[3]John Quincy Adams, "Eulogy on James Madison," in *The Lives of James Madison and James Monroe, Fourth and Fifth Presidents of the United States* (Buffalo, 1851). Douglass Adair cites this source as the first public discussion of *Federalist* No. 10 as a significant, separate essay; see Douglass Adair, *Fame and the Founding Fathers*, ed. Trevor Colbourn (New York, 1974), pp. 78–79.

the principle itself to another place," Publius takes time in No. 9 to clear the ground by citing Montesquieu on republican government. The third "Cato" letter, which had appeared a few weeks earlier in the *New-York Journal*, had quoted that French writer as a celebrated authority on the necessity of small territory for good republican government. "In large republics, the public good is sacrificed to a thousand views; in a small one the interest of the public is easily perceived, better understood, and more within the reach of every citizen; abuses have a less extent, and of course are less protected."[4] This was familiar political doctrine, often repeated by antifederalists. Publius is evidently answering "Cato" directly. He argues that in recommending a small territory Montesquieu had in mind dimensions less than those of most states in America, and he quotes extensively from the *Spirit of Laws* to show that the author actually favored "confederated republics" as a means of "extending the sphere of popular government" and limiting insurrections and local abuses. Then he applies this notion from Montesquieu to the American situation. On the whole, No. 9 is less polished than the paper that follows it. It leans heavily on external materials—"Cato" and Montesquieu—and provides little that is original in thought. It evidently serves as an introduction to No. 10, which further develops the same general idea.

Both papers also fit into a sequential development in the early *Federalist*. Paper No. 1 takes notice of critics who believed that the union would be of "too great extent for any general system." Paper No. 6 cites the Abbé de Mably, who encouraged the formation of confederated republics under firm constitutions. And this group of papers, Nos. 1–14, is marked off as a coherent discussion of the advan-

[4] *The Complete Anti-Federalist*, ed. Herbert J. Storing (Chicago, 1981), II, 110.

tages of union: Nos. 1–2 on general advantages, Nos. 3–5 on advantages in foreign relations, Nos. 6–10 on "dangers . . . from dissensions between the States themselves, and from domestic factions and convulsions" (No. 6). Nos. 6–8 treat dangers between the states; Nos. 9 and 10, dangers of factions within them. The remaining papers take up financial advantages of union, then Publius concludes in No. 14 with further discussion of republican principles and the particular American situation. *Federalist* No. 10 does not stand out from this pattern; rather, it nicely fits into it. The author knows how to carry forward ideas that have already been sketched and anticipated.

Furthermore, this one paper handily illustrates the three strategies of candor which we traced in the run of the whole series. The idea of candor is explicit in the first paragraph (and the word "candid" appears there). The paper makes a very positive argument in favor of union. It is constructed as a rigorous deduction from shining first principles. And along with No. 9, it fully and explicitly answers a leading objection to the Constitution. If Hamilton alone outlined the design of the *Federalist* and planned its opening papers, then it is hard to believe that he did not write No. 10!

There is a curious Hamiltonian sequel to the *Federalist*, too. When Washington was planning his retirement from the presidency he consulted both Hamilton and Madison in writing his Farewell Address. Both men prepared drafts and went over revisions. But it was Hamilton, not Madison, who wrote out a passage containing the doctrine of stable republican government in a large territory. This passage deserves full quotation:

> In republics of narrow extent, it is not difficult for those who at any time possess the reins of administra-

tion, or even for partial combinations of men, who from birth, riches and other sources of distinction have an extraordinary influence by possessing or acquiring the direction of the military force or by sudden efforts of partisans & followers to overturn the established order of things and effect a usurpation,— But in republics of large extent the one or the other is scarcely possible.—The powers and opportunities of resistance of a numerous and wide extended nation defy the successful efforts of the ordinary military force or of any collections [or assemblages] which wealth and patronage may call to their aid—especially if there be no city of overbearing force, resources and influence.[5]

Hamilton's point here is seasoned with thoughts of military force, aristocracy, and powerful cities. But the main outline is still plainly recognizable. Washington omitted this passage from his Address, but it survives as a record of Publius's imprint on Hamilton, a persisting pattern in his thoughts about faction in America.

Hume, Montesquieu, and the *Federalist* Authors

Discussions of the tenth paper took a new direction in 1957, with Douglass Adair's discovery of similar ideas and phrases in essays by David Hume.[6] Close reading con-

---

[5] "Hamilton's Original Major Draft," in Victor Hugh Paltsits, *Washington's Farewell Address* (1935), pp. 189–190, quoted in Theodore Draper, "Hume & Madison: The Secrets of Federalist Paper No. 10," *Encounter*, 58 (February, 1982), 43. Draper also calls attention to a passage in *Federalist* No. 27, claimed by Hamilton, which condenses the main ideas of Nos. 10 and 14 (p. 42).

[6] Douglass Adair, "'That Politics May Be Reduced to a Science': David Hume, James Madison, and the Tenth Federalist," *Huntington Library Quarterly*, 20 (1957), 343–360 (rpt. in *Fame*, pp. 93–106).

vinced Adair that Hume's pages must have lain open next to Madison when he was composing this first contribution to the *Federalist*.

Hume's "Idea of a Perfect Commonwealth" (1752) concludes with a discussion of the ideal size of a republic. "Though it is more difficult to form a republican government in an extensive country than in a city," Hume wrote, "there is more facility, when once it is formed, of preserving it steady and uniform, without tumult or faction." Adair noticed this passage and then called attention to "two sentences that must have electrified Madison when he read them":

> In a large government, which is modelled with masterly skill, there is compass and room enough to refine the democracy, from the lower people, who may be admitted into the first elections or first concoction of the commonwealth, to the higher magistrates, who direct all the movements. At the same time, the parts are so distant and remote, that it is very difficult, either by intrigue, prejudice, or passion, to hurry them into any measures against the public interest.

Here, Adair proclaims, Madison found the source of his own theory of republican government (Adair, *Fame*, pp. 98–100).

Elsewhere in Hume's essays Adair found other words, phrases, and sentences that were exactly transcribed into paper No. 10. He scrutinized Hume's "Parties in General" and found striking similarities of phrase (Hume: "Men have such a propensity to divide into personal factions that the smallest appearance of real difference will produce them"; No. 10: "So strong is this propensity to fall into mutual animosities, that where no substantial occasion presents itself, the most frivolous and fanciful distinctions have been sufficient to kindle their unfriendly passions and excite their most violent conflicts"), common usage of an otherwise obscure term ("aliment"), and similar patterns of ideas and technical vocabulary (Adair, *Fame*, pp. 103–105). In short, Adair points to plenty of solid evidence to clinch his claim of Publius's debt to Hume. His discovery is impossible to overturn. But what does this discovery mean? Hume is yet another author behind this particular issue of the *Federalist*; but what is the significance of this fact? This is the hard, largely unanswerable question.

Adair flatly assumes that Madison alone penned No. 10 and developed his theory from month to month in 1787, by drawing on his own experience of government as well as his scholarly reading. But we have just discussed how No. 10 also carries strong marks of Hamilton's influence. This touch of Hume seems to reinforce that point. Madison hardly mentions Hume elsewhere, never favorably. But Hamilton does refer to Hume and copy some of his phrases. In fact he quotes and acknowledges a long passage from Hume's *Essays* in the very last *Federalist*, No. 85. Did Hume come to Madison's attention by way of Hamilton? Did this *Federalist* paper emerge out of conversations about Hume between these two collaborators? Did Hamilton perhaps leave his own critique of Madison's Convention speech on his partner's desk—as a bookmark, say, on just the right page of Hume's essays? Or did Madison somehow lead Hamilton back to Hume, and force himself to review that author's essays, too? There is no way of knowing.

Clearly the issue here is not mindless copying or plagiarism. Publius copied some things exactly from Hume, but he also drew them into a shape of his own and applied his theory in terms of the immediate American situation. Theodore Draper argues that Hume's name and authority may have been suppressed in No. 10 for two good reasons. One was that Hume was notorious in America as a defender of British monarchy. The other was that his various political essays could be quoted on both sides, in favor of small republics as well as large ones. To name Hume's authority would have been to invite some easy rejoinders.[7] In addition, the circumstances of No. 10 would have worked against a direct citation of sources. The preceding paper, No. 9, points out that Montesquieu himself writes against small republics in the *Spirit of Laws*. It would be anticlimactic to cite Hume against Montesquieu in No. 10. It would also be awkward to name sources and mark quotations in a paper that features such a clear, bare argument from concise definitions and propositions. Finally, the many background papers we have surveyed show that Hamilton and Madison had been weighing the advantages of a large republic in their own terms for months. Hume's words and pages seem to have reinforced their thoughts. Maybe a fresh reading of Hume inspired them to the display, in No. 10, of rigorous philosophical reasoning, but without Hume they might have produced much the same arguments in much the same form.

The presence of Hume, however, gives this essay a certain glamor to modern eyes. As we noticed in Chapter One, Adair himself interpreted his discovery very favorably. If No. 10 is taken as the finest of the *Federalist* essays, and it is also borne in mind that Hume (whom Adair calls the "ablest British philosopher of his age") stands behind it, then it seems to summarize a very great lesson in political philosophy. Publius is not only answering antifederalists here, he is advancing a great theoretical discovery

[7]Draper, "Hume & Madison," pp. 38–40, 43–44.

and publishing it on the eve of its application in the New World.

But is this really the case? Were Hamilton and Madison looking beyond the immediate moment? Did they mean to defeat Montesquieu by revitalizing Hume, and erect American federalism in the light of brilliant theory? It is possible, but I doubt it. For reasons tedious to repeat, it seems more likely that Publius is here answering "Cato" and others with materials readily at hand; that he is contributing a further reason for supporting union among the states; that he is making a conspicuous demonstration of reasoning, but one which he was incapable of maintaining in his own later papers.

Of course, whether or not Hamilton and Madison were fully conscious of it, *Federalist* No. 10 might still be a brilliant presentation of an unassailable idea. But that is another matter, one that extends beyond the authority or influence of Hume.

Publius as Theorist

A year before Adair published his paper on Hume and the *Federalist*, another study took No. 10 very seriously as the outline of a theory of American government. *A Preface to Democratic Theory* by Robert A. Dahl opens with a chapter entitled "Madisonian Democracy," in which this paper is anatomized and discussed as a lasting contribution to American politics. "Madison . . . had the rare gift—doubly rare among political leaders—of lucid, logical, and orderly exposition of his theoretical argument; perhaps in no other political writing by an American is there a more compactly logical, almost mathematical, piece of theory than in Madison's *The Federalist*, No. 10. Hence it is both convenient and intellectually rewarding to turn to Madison to discover a basic rationale for the American political system."[8]

Dahl does hedge a bit about the value of this paper as it stands. He states that Madison was not alone in his thinking, that he was not always as logical, consistent, and explicit as he might have been, and that perhaps in the *Federalist* he was a rhetorician more than a theorist. But in the end he calls the theory he discusses Madisonian and he finds almost all of it in No. 10. "I would be content to let Madison the theorist lie in peace—if it were not for the fact that he so profoundly shaped and shapes American thinking about democracy" (p. 5). Rather than qualifying the theory, Dahl does his best to present it in even more precise form. At the end of his chapter, he summarizes the argument in four basic definitions, one axiom, and a sequence of ten hypotheses! Although he proceeds to find conceptual problems within this scheme, even when so refined, Dahl begins by paying it the tribute of further refinement. He also concludes that for all its faults it is bound to remain a key to American politics. "Whatever its defects of logic, definition, and scientific utility, the Madisonian ideology is likely to remain the most prevalent and deeply rooted of all the styles of thought that might properly be labeled 'American.' One would be foolish indeed to suppose that an examination of its illogicality would significantly diminish its acceptance" (pp. 30–31).

But when Dahl looks closely at the argument he finds a number of serious problems. Many of them have already been mentioned: Publius's failure to specify the rights a minority should preserve, or to specify to what degree

[8]Robert A. Dahl, *A Preface to Democratic Theory* (Chicago, 1956), p. 5.

they must be held inviolable; the impossibility of determining the permanent and aggregate interests of a society; and the failure to take full account of the insidious dangers of minority tyranny. (Some of the latter seem to be the concern of Hamilton's commentary notes from the Convention.) A deeper problem, which Dahl constantly runs up against, is that terms and propositions which seem to have a definite meaning in No. 10 dissolve under close scrutiny. Dahl tries to repair some defects by calling upon definitions and refinements from other *Federalist* papers claimed by Madison. Yet these entail further ambiguities and restrictions. We might expect this, having seen for ourselves how misleading it can be to take any sentence or paragraph from the *Federalist* at face value. But where else is Dahl to turn? He tries Madison's other writings and encounters similar problems. Paper No. 10 does not suffice by itself, and yet a satisfying, fuller development of this tantalizingly compact essay is nowhere to be found.

At the core of his discussion, moreover, Dahl reveals a conceptual problem that separates Publius's doctrine from a long line of political wisdom. The very first propositions that Dahl reconstructs have to do with the importance of external checks on the behavior of men in power. "If unrestrained by external checks, any given individual or group of individuals will tyrannize over others." This exact point is implicit rather than explicit in No. 10, but any reader will allow that Dahl is right to see it there. Dahl's definition of "external check" is also easy to accept. "An 'external check' for any individual consists of the application of rewards and penalties, or the expectation that they will be applied, by some source other than the given individual himself." The important idea here—that men cannot be trusted to check themselves—is surely contained in a crucial pronouncement in No. 10: "No man is allowed to be a judge in his own cause; because his interest would certainly bias his judgment, and, not improbably, corrupt his integrity. With equal, nay with greater reason, a body of men, are unfit to be both judges and parties, at the same time." When Dahl traces the implications of this idea, he finds that it leads to a very barren conception of men and government. Ordinary social sanctions and individual internal checks on behavior are discounted, while the force of government to apply rewards and penalties becomes all-important. Social indoctrination, education, cultural habits—or in Dahl's terms, "family structure, belief systems, myths, heroes, legitimate types of behavior in primary groups, prevailing or modal personality types"—all are ignored in favor of the supposed controls of checks and sanctions in a constitutional republic (p. 18). Dahl allows that Madison and Hamilton knew better. Along with other early-American theorists they knew that virtuous character was the essential basis of ancient political theory and a necessary condition of modern republican government. Dahl concludes that No. 10 is "oversimplified for purposes of debate." But he also quotes Madison's speech of June 6, in which honesty, respect for character, conscience, and religion are specifically rejected as effective checks on majority rule.[9]

On balance, then, Dahl makes much of No. 10, but to

---

[9]Ibid., p. 17. The full passage from Madison is at *PJM*, x, 33. An even fuller discussion of the worthlessness of inner checks is in the memorandum behind this speech, *PJM*, ix, 355–356. Garry Wills's recent book *Explaining America: The Federalist* (Garden City, N.Y., 1981) is largely an attempt to overturn Dahl's analysis by denying the accuracy of its opening propositions concerning external checks. But Wills does not confront these passages from Madison, or Madison's argument at the Convention in favor of an aristocratic Senate. Wills starts from the same assumptions as Dahl's: Madison wrote No. 10 and it is consistent with his other writings. But he is evidently very selective, as well as erudite and penetrating, in discovering and interpreting this consistent Madison.

do so he has to strain the text itself, seek support from other *Federalist* papers and writings by Hamilton and Madison, admit insoluble difficulties in the paper's logic, and fall back on patient allowances for rhetorical distortions or antiquated conceptions. He has to discover, manipulate, or choose among contexts in which the paper makes complete sense, and justify such labors of scholarship with a self-fulfilling assumption—that No. 10, whether or not it is intellectually defensible, is somehow deeply engraved in the minds and hearts of Americans.

This same problem confronts anyone who tries to expound the inner truth of this single paper. The effort is bound to be somewhat self-defeating. The apparent beauty of the paper is its self-contained lucidity, its open, specific, compact discussion of a palpable problem before ordinary citizens. But any close analysis reveals intellectual problems and intellectual subtleties. Full explication attracts and exercises the talents of a scholar—and so lands him in the uncomfortable task of spinning a tortuous web out of fine Euclidean principles or hauling vast tomes of learning and cross-reference in order to buttress an apparently solid arch. Dahl is not the only serious modern commentator on this celebrated paper. Far from it. But his work is as intelligent, patient, and appreciative as any, and it fully illustrates this paradox.

It also succeeds in moving beyond it. Dahl is quite aware of the double thrust of his analysis—to celebrate the importance of No. 10 and at the same time to demolish its claims to clarity and coherence. He solves this problem by looking to larger contexts than authorship, sources, and the debates of 1787. He asks why this paper now makes such a lasting impression. And so he turns to the constant need of Americans for a rationalization that explains how minorities are protected under majority rule:

At the formation of the Constitution, the Madisonian style of argument provided a satisfying, persuasive, and protective ideology for the minorities of wealth, status, and power, who distrusted and feared their bitter enemies—the artisans and farmers of inferior wealth, status, and power, who they thought 'constituted the "popular majority." Today, however, it seems probable that for historically explicable reasons a preponderant number of politically active Americans believe themselves to be members, at least part of the time, of one or more minorities—minorities, moreover, whose goals might be threatened if the prescribed constitutional authority of majorities were legally unlimited. [p. 30]

Whatever its shortcomings as a theory, this paper still carries a satisfying authority. It meets a need. It seems to explain in intellectual terms what is already felt as an achievement in American life. And of course it is also a document dating from the foundation of the Constitution and ratified by two centuries of political stability. It fails as what it seems to be—a presentation of hard theory. But it is bound to survive as a venerable statement of practical wisdom concerning minority rights under majority rule.

Publius as Prophetic Ethnographer

Dahl's shrewd suggestion that the force of No. 10 lies in a present need for it rather than in its own coherence or historical setting is seconded by a curious fact. Until the twentieth century, this single issue was hardly noticed at all. It was Charles Beard's *An Economic Interpretation of the Constitution of the United States* (1913) that first isolated this paper and made much of its precise logic. Beard called No.

10 "the most philosophical examination of the foundations of political science" and he quoted from it extensively (though very selectively and sometimes inaccurately) to prove that the Founders planned a government that would protect propertied interests against the democracy of "the landless proletariat."[10]

Most later commentaries have been written under the long shadow of Beard's influence, though often in direct rebuttal of his conclusions. What is more, the most thorough scholarly work on the *Federalist* dates from the end of the Second World War, that is, from the time when the United States emerged as a consolidated, continental nation and a great power in the world. Adair, Dahl, the modern editors of Madison and Hamilton, and a dozen other critics of the *Federalist* have all labored under a modern pressure to explain America to the world, to rediscover the roots of modern democracy, to define the prospects of world federalism, or to popularize the idealism of the American way. These aims are worthwhile in themselves, but they make the modern celebrity of No. 10 a rather suspect phenomenon.

It is odd, for example, that this paper never achieved great fame or discussion during the long decades of continental exploration and expansion. One might suppose that a doctrine that rested on the slogan "expand the sphere" would coincide handily with the ideas of Manifest Destiny. But so far as I can tell, no one ever made much of it. Adair specifically looked for any such use of No. 10 before 1913 and found very little (*Fame*, pp. 78–82). Yet one modern reader wildly claims that its basic doctrine, favoring large republics, lies behind the Louisiana Purchase, wars with

---

[10] Charles A. Beard, *An Economic Interpretation of the Constitution of the United States* (1913, rev. ed. 1935; rpt. New York, 1965), pp. 156–157.

Mexico and Spain, and expansion across the Pacific. "Thus the issue which Madison attacked frontally in No. 10 set the United States on a course which stretches from that day to this. What began as a rationale for the domestic tranquillity, common defense, general welfare and the blessings of liberty for thirteen states ended by extending the reach of the republic to 50 states and 'world power.' From this point of view, No. 10 is still very much with us."[11]

No. 10 also seems "still very much with us" in another sense, which reaches beyond politics, history, and historiography. After two centuries, the doctrine of minority rights has become so ingrained in American society that it now reaches into the rhythms of personal life. And as a result, this *Federalist* paper now turns out to mirror a describable condition of modern American cultural identity.

In 1950 Erik Erikson published *Childhood and Society*, a book that has become a classic of Freudian psychiatry, a thorough introduction to human development and the subtle indoctrination that children receive from the societies into which they must grow. At the end of the book Erikson presents a chapter called "Reflections on the American Identity." He brings to this subject several advantages of his own experience: birth and education abroad, clinical training and expertise, long association with active anthropologists, years of practice with children in several regions of the United States, and recent work with soldiers making painful readjustments from the brutality of war. Most to the purpose, he bases his remarks on direct observations and a broad reading of historical forces, not on pedantic principles; and he approaches the well-worn sub-

[11] Draper, "Hume & Madison," p. 36.

ject of American identity with refreshing skepticism and self-awareness.[12]

His remarks directly touch the doctrines we have been surveying. "In this country," he writes, "the image of the freeman is founded on that northern European who, having escaped feudal and religious laws, disavowed his motherland and established a country and a constitution on the prime principle of preventing the resurgence of autocracy" (p. 304). And he goes on to discuss how this prime principle has been modified by American conditions.

When he comes to the American family, Erikson finds a remarkable pattern. Autocracy is suppressed, and as a result more democratic forces affect every daily activity. "The American family," he says, "tends to guard the right of the individual member—parents included—not to be dominated. In fact, each member, as he grows and changes, reflects a variety of outside groups and their changing interests and needs: the father's occupational group, the mother's club, the adolescent's clique, and the children's first friends. These interest groups determine the individual's privileges in his family; it is they who judge the family." Erikson makes a partial exception for the American mother. She seems to remain above parties and interests; but that is because it is her role "to see to it that each party and interest develops as vigorously as possible—up to the point where she must put in a veto in the interest of another individual or of the family as a whole."

Here, then, we must expect to find the inner rationale for a variety of activities and inactivities: they represent not so much what everybody wants to do, but

[12] Erik H. Erikson, *Childhood and Society*, 2d ed. (New York, 1963), pp. 285–325.

rather what, of all the available things to do, is least unacceptable to anybody concerned. Such an inner arrangement, of course, is easily upset by any show of vested interest, or special interest, or minority interest: and it is for this reason that there is a great amount of apparently petty bickering whenever interests clash. The family is successful if the matter is settled to the point of "majority concurrence," even if this is reluctantly given; it is gradually undermined by frequent decisions in favor of one interest group, be it the parents or the babies. This give-and-take cuts down to an extraordinary degree the division of the family into unequal partners who can claim privileges on the basis of age, strength, weakness, or goodness. Instead, the family becomes a training ground in the tolerance of different *interests*—not of different *beings*; liking and loving has little to do with it. In fact, both overt loving and overt hating are kept on a low key, for either might weaken the balance of the family and the chances of the individual member: for the over-all important thing is to accrue claims for future privilege justifiable on the basis of one's past concessions. [pp. 316–317]

Erikson finds in this family situation a matrix for the prevention of autocracy and inequality. "It makes complete irresponsibility impossible, and it makes open hate and warfare in families rare." And it makes it impossible for uncompromising ideology to take root in American life (p. 318).

Erikson does not describe this pattern in order to praise it. He worries about the failures of authority and energy that such constant compromising can breed. He also accounts for this pattern by referring to forces different from the Constitution. The rejected autocracies of political and religious life have been replaced by other autocracies in

America. One is the daunting geography of a vast continent. "The size and rigor of the country and the importance of the means of migration and transportation helped to create and to develop the identity of autonomy and initiative, the identity of him who is 'going places and doing things.' Historically the overdefined past was apt to be discarded for the undefined future; geographically, migration was an ever-present fact; socially, chances and opportunities lay in daring and luck, in taking full advantage of the channels of social motility" (pp. 304–305). And coupled with this pressure to hold oneself ready for change and advancement has been the autocracy of the machine—not only the hard metallic surroundings of factories and railroads, but the standards of timeclock punctuality and mass-produced tastes. Both these forces, Erikson feels, push the family to suppress strong ties or authorities and to encourage loose-knit compromises, fostering the understanding that children must grow up to move on and that powers outside the home will determine the individual's sense of belonging.

In other words, Erikson seems to have discovered the principles of *Federalist* No. 10—emphasis on minority rights, interest groups, the compromise discovery of permanent and aggregate interests—by looking at current family life and at historical forces that emerged long after 1787. He does point to an analogous situation in politics. "Now it is an unwritten but firm rule of Congress that no important bloc shall ever be voted down—under normal circumstances—on any matter which touches its own vital interests" (p. 316). But here he is quoting a political discussion in a popular magazine, and the stress is on an *unwritten* rule, a developed habit rather than an articulate principle.[13]

[13] Erikson quotes John Fischer, "Unwritten Rules of American Politics," *Harper's Magazine*, 197 (November 1948), 27–36. Fischer ac-

What matters for Erikson is childhood, psychological development, and education, not political theory.

Has *Federalist* No. 10 therefore exerted a subtle and penetrating influence, so that today even the child in the cradle feels its effects? Did Publius see so well into the Constitution that he shrewdly prophesied a way of life? The more reasonable conclusion is that modern America has found in No. 10 an apt reflection of later developments—that No. 10 has been singled out because of modern folkways rather than that modern America has emerged because of No. 10.

This state of affairs marks a startling twist in the history of the *Federalist*. As we have noticed at many points, these papers represent and encourage a wholly new departure from illiterate, familiar reliance on timeworn habits in society. Dahl specifically scores No. 10 for ignoring such sanctions as "family structure, belief systems, myths, heroes." Old Amos Singletary had strong fears of a constitution that rested on positive law in place of religious faith. Publius himself pointed to the ratification process as a rare moment of enlightened decision for mankind. Yet with the passage of time this dangerous new departure has become a hallowed precedent. If Erikson is at all right in his analysis of American family character, and if we are correct in seeing No. 10 as an apt expression of this modern situation, then the authority of this paper has changed completely. Instead of justifying a new government on the basis of hard, cold logic and high principle, it now explains and symbolizes a government so long accepted as to be

---

knowledges heavy indebtedness to Peter F. Drucker, whose discussion of Calhoun's pluralism appeared in the *Review of Politics* (October 1948) and is reprinted in his *Men, Ideas, & Politics* (New York, 1971), pp. 105–125. Drucker discusses two of John C. Calhoun's political treatises, which were not published until after his death in 1852. Neither Fischer nor Drucker mentions Madison or the *Federalist*.

worn smooth, worn into the flesh and blood of generations. The patina of its oldness and clarity seems to support
the ways of continental expansion and safe democratic
bickering, but its solid core of rational daring has utterly
vanished.

Of course it is hard to gainsay this new source of authority. The combination of easily blurred details concerning this paper—its composite authorship by Hamilton and
Madison, its occasion at the beginning of the Constitution,
its extreme lucidity—are bound to stir the interest of an
American reader. And the fact that its arguments nicely coincide with observable modern conditions makes it all the
more fascinating. It may be impossible to dislodge a common reader's easy conclusion that these two authorities
must merge. *Federalist* No. 10 may just be an indelible
monument in the American imagination—like the supposed signing of the Declaration of Independence on the
Fourth of July, to the ringing of the Liberty Bell.

But truth is truth, and there is a disparity between this
paper as it has become and its power as part of the *Federalist*
series. What both versions share is shining clarity and an
appeal to the minds of common citizen-readers. But by
itself this is not enough. Modern government cannot rest
on this one slender, incomplete, ambiguous column of
argument.

Conclusion

It may seem that much of this study has been devoted to criticizing the *Federalist* and denying the strong claims made for it by most modern editors and scholars. I have tried to stress that this is a necessary labor, the first step toward understanding a work that still deserves great fame and authority.

The large difference I have tried to expound is finally a difference in attitude on the part of a reader. If one searches for careful philosophy, definitive theory, or a consistent political outlook, the *Federalist* will prove very satisfying— to a point. Thereafter the closer one looks the more frustrating its pages become. Its authors do not remain consistent with each other, or with themselves. Its separate papers do not clash obviously, but neither do they hang together with satisfying exactness. Nevertheless, these papers do remain very consistent if one looks upon them as efforts of active statesmanship, as high political rhetoric.

The difference can be summarized as that between political doctrine and political literature.

Like any work of literature the *Federalist* has a form. It can be compared to other writings of a similar type, the pseudonymous serial essays on politics which shaped public discourse in the eighteenth century. The *Federalist* not only fits into this general category, it enlarges its importance. This work makes use of commonplace features—hidden authorship, collaborative refinement of arguments, appeal to a new generation of newspaper readers—but it also transforms them. Its authors' full preparation and effort, and their sense of the great occasion they were addressing, make this the deepest and most elaborate public discussion of constitutional matters ever circulated. Their awareness of conscientious opposition is reflected in a unique tone of respectful, serious, generous, full argument. Altogether these eighty-five papers stand out as a brilliant exercise of freedom of the press, a bright culmination of decades of developing journalism.

Like any work of literature, the *Federalist* demands rereading. In part this is a consequence of its form, or forms: a book which is a collection of newspaper essays, or rather essays that were published in newspapers and then collected between hard covers in two volumes. Each single paper makes one sort of sense by itself, another as part of the series. But deeper than this is the play throughout the *Federalist* of two strong minds, each still growing in its own comprehension of the Constitution. Later papers not only depend on earlier ones, and enlarge them, they also reconsider and redefine them. The whole enterprise reflects a dynamic interplay of challenges and answers, promises scrupulously kept, and outlines modified by growth.

Like any work of literature the *Federalist* has its own integrity. It cannot adequately be explained by reference to something else: the intentions of the founders, the biography of James Madison, the debates in Philadelphia, or the Constitution. It is more than the sum of its influences and contexts. And of course it is more than the sum of its parts;

it resists dismemberment. It is not fairly represented by No. 10, No. 51, and No. 78 any more than *Hamlet* is fairly summarized in a ghost story, Polonius's advice to Laertes, and the poetry of the soliloquies.

Finally, like any work of literature the *Federalist* repays close study with a special authority. It endures through time and addresses new generations on its own terms, not merely with the antique noises of long-forgotten axioms or the chance pertinence of certain quotations for passing modern causes. The authority of Publius does not lie in indelible pronouncements from the Father of the Constitution. Rather it demonstrates that such things do not exist, and that active, civilized, public debate is better in every way.

Index

Adair, Douglass, 31n, 41–42, 56–58,
 126n, 129–132, 139
Adams, John, 43, 86n, 90, 103
Adams, John Quincy, 126
Addison, Joseph, 89–91, 94
American Revolution, 68, 70–71,
 86n, 92
Annapolis, 93
Articles of Confederation, 22, 46, 57,
 69–74, 92, 106
Authority, 22, 80–97, 110–111
 defined, 80, 87

Bagehot, Walter, 95
Bancroft, George, 56n
Beard, Charles A., 39–42, 138–139
Bible, 104–111
Bill of Rights, 27, 57
Bourne, Edward G., 31n
"Brutus," 49, 51–52, 63
Butler, Samuel, 104n

"Caesar," 48–49, 51–52
Calhoun, John C., 144n
Candor:
 defined, 62–64
 strategies of, 52–53, 69–79, 94–97,
 128
"Cato" (New York essay series), 48–
 49, 51–52, 63, 76n, 78, 127, 133
"Cato" (Trenchard and Gordon series), 90
Chase, Samuel, 51

Clinton, George, 21, 23, 46–49
Constitution, United States, 17, 22
 relation to the Federalist papers,
 19–23, 33–39, 43, 58, 75–78,
 93, 147
Constitutional Convention. See Massachusetts Ratifying Convention,
 New York State Ratifying Convention, Philadelphia Convention, Virginia Ratifying
 Convention
Cooke, Jacob E., 31, 49n
Coxe, Tench, 26, 63n

Dahl, Robert A., 133–139, 144
Daily Advertiser, 46–48, 51–53, 55,
 114
Declaration of Independence, 17, 37–
 38, 62, 73, 145
De Pauw, Linda Grant, 46n, 49n
Dickinson, John, 43, 90
Douglas, Stephen A., 95
Draper, Theodore, 129n, 131–132,
 139–140
Duer, William, 54, 60

Erikson, Erik H., 140–144

Faction, theories of, 66–68, 114–145
Federalist (political label), 50–51
Federalist papers:
 authorship of, 23–32, 53–61
 design of, 20–21, 49–53, 147

Index

Federalist papers (*continued*)
distribution of, 20–23, 82–84
effectiveness of, 19–23, 81–84
as philosophy, 39–43, 87, 132–138
publication schedule of, 19, 55,
58–59
as statement of Founders' ideals,
32–39, 84–87
Federalist Party, 38, 94
Ford, Paul L., 31n
Franklin, Benjamin, 89, 91, 96
Frederick, duke of York, 102
Freedom of the press. *See* Journalism

Gideon, Jacob, 28, 30, 56
Gordon, Thomas, 90

Hamilton, Alexander:
claims to authorship of the *Federalist*,
23–32, 45–61, 81–86, 124–129
correspondence and other writings
quoted, 24, 26, 29, 82, 125,
128–129
as delegate in Philadelphia, 24, 33,
47, 54–55, 96, 124–126
in New York politics, 23, 33
Hamilton, John C., 27–28, 31n, 55
Hayne, Robert, 35
"Helvidius," 28, 34
Hopkins, George F., 27–28
Hume, David, 41–42, 74, 106–107,
113, 129–133

Independent Journal, 51–53

Jay, John, 21, 26–27, 53–54, 56–60,
81, 86n, 103
Jefferson, Thomas, 43, 86n, 103, 108
correspondence with James Madison, 24–27, 37–39, 121
Johnson, Samuel, 62, 89, 95
Johnson, William Samuel, 55
Journalism:
as a democratic institution, 82,
87–97, 147
in New York City, 20–21, 51–53
"Junius," 90–91

King, Rufus, 54–55, 86n

Lansing, John, 47
Letters from the Federal Farmer, 51, 63,
83

Lincoln, Abraham, 95, 103
Literacy:
as antidemocratic, 98–111
rates in New York State, 20–21
Lodge, Henry Cabot, 31n
Lycurgus, 67

Mably, L'Abbé Gabriel Bonne de, 127
McLean, Archibald, 55
Madison, James:
on authority of the *Federalist*,
25–30, 34–39
claims to authorship of the *Federalist*, 23–32, 54–61, 77, 84–86,
118–124
correspondence and other writings
quoted, 22, 25, 26–29, 34–36,
38, 55–56, 60, 82–83, 85, 89, 96,
119–121
as a delegate in Philadelphia, 25,
35–36, 54–59, 96, 119–121, 136
Marshall, John, 95
Mason, Alpheus, 31n
Massachusetts Bill of Rights, 108
Massachusetts Ratifying Convention,
71, 98–111
Montesquieu, Charles de Secondat,
113, 127, 132–133
Morris, Gouverneur, 54–55, 58, 60,
103
Mosteller, Frederick, 31–32, 49n

Newspapers. *See* Journalism; *entries for
individual newspapers; entries for in-
dividual essay series (e.g., "Caesar")*
New-York Journal, 21, 48, 55, 82, 99n,
127
New York Legislature, 19, 20
New-York Morning Post, 51–52, 109
New-York Packet, 51–53, 55
New York Ratifying Convention, 19,
22, 107

Otto, Louis G., 21, 46n

"Pacificus," 28, 34
Paine, Thomas, 90
Philadelphia Convention, 81, 84–85,
102
Hamilton's and Madison's participation in, 17, 24–25, 33, 41,
46–48, 54–57, 119–121,
124–126

Index

Madison's records of, 35–36, 58–59, 96, 119–121
mentioned in the *Federalist*, 65, 67–69
and press freedom, 93–96
Pierce, William, 54–55
Plutarch, 51
Pound, Ezra, 110
Publius (Roman statesman), 51

Randolph, Edmund, 55, 60, 82
Randolph, John, 26
Republican Party, 37–38, 94
Revolution. *See* American Revolution; Shays's Rebellion
Rush, Benjamin, 26, 103

Schuyler, Philip, 86n
Self-evidence, 72–74
Shays's Rebellion, 100
Singletary, Amos, 98–111, 144
Smith, Jonathan, 100–111
Smith, Melancton, 23n
Solon, 51, 67
Storing, Herbert J., 49n, 51n
Stuart, Archibald, 26n
Swift, Jonathan, 89–90

Trenchard, John, 90

Union, advantages of, 58, 69–71

Virginia Plan, 54
Virginia Ratifying Convention, 22, 23, 95
Virginia State Constitutional Convention (1829), 34–35
Virginia Statute of Religious Liberty, 108
Virginia, University of, 37–38

Wallace, David L., 31–32, 49n
Washington, George, 22, 34, 47–48, 66, 81, 86, 103
correspondence of, 26, 59–60, 82
Farewell Address of, 128–129
Webster, Daniel, 35
White, Morton, 73–74
Wilkes, John, 90–94
Wills, Garry, 136n

Yates, Abraham, 47
York, duke of. *See* Frederick, duke of York

Library of Congress Cataloging in Publication Data

Furtwangler, Albert, 1942–
    The authority of Publius.

    Includes index.
    1. Federalist.   I. Title.
JK155.F87   1984   342.73'024   83-18806
ISBN 0-8014-1643-4 (alk. paper) 347.30224